Never Say Die

NEVER SAY DIE

*A Kentucky Colt,
the Epsom Derby,
and the Rise
of the Modern
Thoroughbred Industry*

JAMES C. NICHOLSON

FOREWORD BY PETE BEST

UNIVERSITY PRESS OF KENTUCKY

Scholarly publisher for the Commonwealth,
serving Bellarmine University, Berea College, Centre College of
Kentucky, Eastern Kentucky University, The Filson Historical Society,
Georgetown College, Kentucky Historical Society, Kentucky State
University, Morehead State University, Murray State University,
Northern Kentucky University, Transylvania University, University of
Kentucky, University of Louisville, and Western Kentucky University.
All rights reserved.

Editorial and Sales Offices: The University Press of Kentucky
663 South Limestone Street, Lexington, Kentucky 40508-4008
www.kentuckypress.com

17 16 15 14 13   5 4 3 2 1

Library of Congress Cataloging-in-Publication Data

Nicholson, James C.
  Never Say Die : a Kentucky colt, the Epsom Derby, and the rise of
the modern Thoroughbred industry / James C. Nicholson ; foreword
by Pete Best.
      pages cm
  Includes bibliographical references and index.
   ISBN 978-0-8131-4167-1 (hardcover : alk. paper) —
   ISBN 978-0-8131-4200-5 (epub) — ISBN 978-0-8131-4201-2 (pdf)
   1. Derby (Horse race)—History—20th century. 2. Horse racing—
England—History—20th century. 3. England—Social life and
customs—20th century. 4. Never Say Die (Race horse) I. Title.
SF357.E67N53 2013
798.400942—dc23   2012051377

This book is printed on acid-free paper meeting the requirements of
the American National Standard for Permanence in Paper for Printed
Library Materials.

Manufactured in the United States of America.

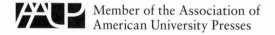 Member of the Association of
American University Presses

To my parents,
Joe Browne and Jessica Nicholson

Contents

Illustrations

Foreword

A Victorian house . . . a racehorse . . . jewelry . . . a rock band. Sounds like the basic ingredients for a good book. Interested? Read on. Who would have thought that a bet placed on a racehorse would influence the course of popular music and the sport of Thoroughbred racing? You don't believe it? Well, it's true. I was there.

My mother, Mona Best, pawned all her jewelry and bet on a horse called Never Say Die, ridden by a young jockey named Lester Piggott, to win the 1954 English Derby. The horse won at the magnificent payoff of 33–1. With the winnings Mona bought a spacious Victorian house at 8 Haymans Green in Liverpool, the cellars of which she turned into the world-famous Casbah Coffee Club. The Casbah became the catalyst for the Mersey beat sound and was a springboard for the Beatles. The rest, you might say, is history, because the Beatles went on to become the biggest icons of the music industry and the most successful group in history.

Never Say Die's Derby victory, which was so important to my family and to the career of the Beatles, also had a major impact on the sport of Thoroughbred racing, which you will learn about in this book. In these pages you will encounter a wide cast of characters, including Never Say Die's owner, trainer, and jockey, as well as many others who had a hand in raising and racing the horse that made history.

Since that fateful day when Never Say Die won the Derby, his name has become the war cry of the Best family. To us it means courage, inspiration, and determination. It has been the driving force during my generation, and I am certain that "Never Say Die" will ring out in the households of future generations of the Best family. These three little words mean so much to my family and me. Read on to learn what the horse by that name has meant to history.

Pete Best
Original drummer of the Beatles

Preface

Within Thoroughbred racing literature, the "outstanding race-horse biography" is a familiar subgenre. The 1954 Epsom Derby champion Never Say Die was a very good racehorse, but, depending on one's definition of greatness, he was arguably not historically great. His exploits on the racecourse would not, in and of themselves, justify a book-length biography. But this book is not a traditional biography of a horse. Rather, Never Say Die is the unifying element in a collection of stories and characters that illuminates the economic, social, political, and cultural forces responsible for the development of the American Thoroughbred and the creation of the modern international Thoroughbred industry.

In the twentieth century, as the United States became the wealthiest and most influential nation in the world, the center of power within the sport of horse racing shifted from Britain to the United States. As new American wealth brought the top European bloodstock to the United States, American Thoroughbreds—long derided by Europeans as completely inferior to their stock—became the most sought-after and valuable animals on earth, transforming Thoroughbred racing and breeding from an aristocratic sporting pursuit into the multibillion-dollar industry it is today.

At its best, the sport of horse racing unites people who would have little in common but for their affection for the Thoroughbred. This book weaves together a wide range of seemingly disparate characters, including a bigamous failed actor–turned–

inventor, a Muslim imam, an accused treasonist, and the most successful rock-and-roll band of all time. Taken as a whole, these stories and characters illuminate and illustrate the events, conditions, and processes that gave rise to the modern Thoroughbred industry.

Finally, it is appropriate to mention that one of the major players in this story, John A. Bell III, is my maternal grandfather. I believe that I have maintained an objective perspective, but that will be for a forewarned reader to decide.

Chapter 1

A Historic Derby Triumph and a Wager That Changed History

A quarter million people braved the cold and damp conditions at Epsom Downs on June 2, 1954, to witness the 175th running of the Derby Stakes, one of grandest scenes in all of sport. Bentleys and Rolls-Royces, bicycles and motorcycles brought Britons from every background to the racecourse, less than fifteen miles south of central London. Among the throng was Queen Elizabeth II, who hoped her colt Landau could improve on his stablemate Aureole's second-place finish in the previous year's Derby. Prime Minister Sir Winston Churchill adjourned a cabinet meeting early so he could attend the festivities. With the surrounding countryside open to the public, a broad spectrum of humanity that included gypsies, touts, gamblers, and fortune-tellers filled the area around the racecourse, contributing to a spectacle unlike any other on earth. Aristocrats drank champagne, while farmers and laborers ate fish and chips and jellied eels and winkles. Carousels and caravans dotted the landscape as last-minute bets were placed while the field of twenty-two three-year-olds made its way to the starting post.

The racing fans gathered at Epsom were participating in a tradition with deep local roots that traced back to the year 1618, when a serious drought forced a local herdsman named Hen-

1

ry Wicker to look for water for his cattle. He found some in a small hole in the ground on the commons outside what was then the small village of Epsom. Wicker used a spade to widen what turned out to be a spring, creating a large watering area, but his cattle would not drink. He tasted the water and discovered the reason: it was sulfuric mineral water. Eventually, Epsom salts were produced there, and the village became a popular spa destination for rich Londoners who wanted to experience the supposed healing properties of the water. Horse racing soon became part of a culture of leisure at Epsom. King Charles II made the Epsom races a regular royal destination following the Restoration of the English monarchy in 1660, which replaced the culturally restrictive Protectorate, and the well-to-do soon followed in droves.[1]

The Derby Stakes itself had its origins in the inaugural running of the Oaks Stakes for three-year-old fillies at Epsom in 1779. The Oaks was named after the racing lodge of the 12th Earl of Derby, Edward Stanley, who leased the building—a renovated former alehouse—from his uncle by marriage, General John Burgoyne (of American Revolutionary War fame). Following a victory by his filly Bridget in the first Oaks Stakes, the lord held a celebration at his lodge. There, the guests agreed that there should be a similar race organized for colts.[2] According to legend, Lord Derby won a coin flip with influential racing official and member of Parliament Sir Charles Bunbury to determine whose name that race would carry. The following year the first Derby Stakes was held, and it was Bunbury who took the winner's purse with his outstanding colt Diomed. By supporting racing, Bunbury was carrying on something of a family tradition, in that he was married to a great-granddaughter of King Charles II (her grandfather was the illegitimate son of Charles and his mistress, Louise de Kerouvalle).[3]

One hundred seventy-four years later, a chestnut colt called Never Say Die—his name an allusion to a near-death experience

With Never Say Die's victory in the 1954 Epsom Derby, Robert Sterling Clark became the second American owner to win the historic race with an American-born horse. *Portrait of Robert Sterling Clark* (1919), by Emile Friant (French, 1863–1932); pencil on paper, 21¾ by 16½ inches. (Image 1955.742, © Sterling and Francine Clark Art Institute, Williamstown, Massachusetts; photo by Michael Agee)

at birth—took the lead in the final quarter mile beneath eighteen-year-old jockey Lester Piggott and galloped on to a two-length Derby triumph at odds of 33–1, to the astonishment of the hundreds of thousands in attendance and the millions listening to the BBC radio broadcast. With that victory, the colt became the first Kentucky-born horse to win England's great race, and his owner, a "completely flabbergasted" Robert Sterling Clark, became the first American owner to win the race with an American horse he had bred himself.[4] Never Say Die made newspaper headlines on both sides of the Atlantic, and the most earth-shattering part of the story was that the winner of the Epsom Derby had been foaled in the United States and was owned by an American. In the Derby's long history, only one other American-born horse had won—Pennsylvania-bred Iroquois in 1881. No horse born in Kentucky, the commercial breeding center of the American Thoroughbred industry, had ever won the great race.[5]

American horsemen were overjoyed at the news that an American horse had won the Derby. In the *Thoroughbred Record*, a Kentucky-based weekly publication, columnist Frank Jennings noted that, prior to Never Say Die's victory,

> repeated failure on the part of Americans in the English Derby not only was becoming monotonous but was downright discouraging. Men of less determination and means than Mr. Clark gradually had become reconciled to the idea that a score in the big race at Epsom was virtually impossible with a colt bred and raised on this side of the Atlantic. Never Say Die did a great deal toward changing this thought and at the same time provided a fine example of the fact that American bloodlines, when properly blended with those of foreign lands, can hold their own in the top company of the world.[6]

To English horsemen, whose belief in the unfailing superiority of English bloodstock was deeply ingrained, Never Say Die's victory was noteworthy but could be dismissed as an anomaly. But Jennings predicted that Never Say Die's surprise win was a harbinger of future American success: "In this day and age of a smaller world, due to jet flight and whatnot, it is encouraging to realize that the years of almost immediate future might see other American 'invaders' in the winners' circle reserved for the immortals at Epsom."[7]

England was where Thoroughbreds had been developed in the late seventeenth and early eighteenth centuries by breeding stallions from the Middle East to English mares, and Englanders believed that their superiority on the turf was something akin to a divine right. In hindsight, however, Never Say Die's victory in England's most popular race was an early sign of a seismic shift in the world of Thoroughbred racing that would irrevocably alter the global balance of power in the sport.

Never Say Die's seventy-six-year-old owner, heir to an

enormous sewing machine fortune, had lived a remarkable life. Robert Sterling Clark had served as a U.S. Army officer in the Philippines during the Spanish-American War and in China during the Boxer Rebellion, financed and led a research expedition through rural China, and built one of the finest private collections of European painting masterpieces in the world. He was even alleged to have been involved at the highest levels in a plot to overthrow President Franklin D. Roosevelt during the Great Depression. But nothing provided him with greater satisfaction than that historic win in the Epsom Derby. In a statement to the press, Clark called the achievement "the crowning glory of thirty-five years of efforts in thoroughbred breeding."[8]

The winning owner was unable to attend the race in person and received word of the result via a telephone call from his bloodstock adviser. Clark was in a New York City hospital "just having a checkup," according to his secretary.[9] An impromptu champagne celebration was quickly organized in the hospital room, and Clark proposed a series of toasts. The small gathering, which included his lawyer, racing adviser, personal secretary, and wife, first drank to teenaged jockey Lester Piggott, the rising star who piloted Never Say Die. This was the first of what would be a record nine Derby Stakes wins for Piggott, who was destined to enjoy one of the greatest careers in the long history of English racing. They raised their glasses to Joe Lawson, Never Say Die's seventy-three-year-old trainer, who had won most of England's top races but for whom the Derby had proved elusive over a long and accomplished career—until that afternoon. Then they saluted John A. Bell III, the young Kentucky horseman whose fast thinking had helped the colt survive a difficult birth and at whose farm outside Lexington Never Say Die had been raised and introduced to a saddle. For Bell, born into a wealthy Pittsburgh family that lost its banking and coal fortune amid scandal when he was still a child, the Derby victory provided a critical piece of positive publicity for his fledgling equine operation, which would eventually become one of the most respected in the world.

The hospital-room revelers toasted everyone they could think of who had been associated with Never Say Die's historic Derby win. But from a historical perspective, they left at least one important person off their list: Isaac Merritt Singer—the man whose sewing machine gave rise to the first American multinational corporation and to Robert Sterling Clark's immense fortune. Without his inherited wealth, Clark might not have been able to race and breed his top-class Thoroughbreds. And, on a deeper level, the vast American wealth created by Singer and other captains of industry and finance in the late nineteenth and early twentieth centuries made the importation of top European stallions—such as Never Say Die's sire Nasrullah—possible.

Meanwhile, at his estate on the French Riviera, the immensely wealthy and mysterious Aga Khan—spiritual leader of 15 million Ismaili Muslims—also celebrated quietly as he convalesced after a months-long commemoration of his Platinum Jubilee. The festivities had concluded in a gathering at Karachi, where he was ceremonially presented with his weight in the precious metal by an assemblage of his followers in a specially built 50,000-seat stadium. The Aga Khan had won the Derby himself as an owner a record five times. But Never Say Die's victory gave him a different kind of personal satisfaction. The colt's sire, the talented but temperamental Nasrullah, had been bred and raced by the Aga Khan; he had also raced the stallion's mother and grandmother. Nasrullah represented the culmination of a lifelong love of horses and decades of involvement in equine racing and breeding for the imam. The stallion's bloodlines would leave an indelible mark on the Thoroughbred breed and industry around the world. Nasrullah's move from Europe to the United States at the middle of the twentieth century was part of a larger trend: American horsemen, armed with cash from American industrialists and titans of finance, were buying top stallions from across Europe and importing them to the United States, dramatically altering the global balance of power within the Thoroughbred industry in the process.

In Liverpool, 230 miles northwest of Epsom Downs, a middle-class housewife named Mona Best listened to the BBC broadcast of the 1954 Derby on the family radio. When the final results were announced, she literally jumped for joy. Mona had pawned her jewelry in order to place a bet on Never Say Die because she "liked its name and what it stood for."[10] With her winnings, Mona put a down payment on her dream home, a large fifteen-room Victorian at 8 Haymans Green in the West Derby section of Liverpool. Before it was fixed up, her children called it "Dracula's Castle." But it had an unusually spacious cellar consisting of seven rooms, which Mona renovated and turned into the Casbah Coffee Club.

The idea to operate a coffee bar in her basement came to Mona when her son's friends began to flock to the Bests' house after school to listen to American rock-and-roll records by Chuck Berry, Little Richard, Jerry Lee Lewis, Carl Perkins, and Eddie Cochran.[11] "My home was beginning to resemble a railway station at [the] time," Mona later recalled. "There was always someone passing through. My original idea had been to start a little exclusive club for Peter and his friends in the cellars and thus put an end to all this trooping in and out of the living quarters. But within days the word had gone around and young people—most of them complete strangers—began to knock at my front door asking if they could join! There could never have been so much enthusiasm for a club that hadn't yet opened."[12] By opening night, the club had 1,000 members who had paid an annual fee of 12½ pence each.

A group of teenaged musicians called the Quarrymen played at the club's opening night, August 29, 1959, after helping to paint the walls and the ceilings.[13] The name of the group came from the Quarry Bank Grammar School in Liverpool, which the band's leader had attended. He was John Lennon. Paul McCartney, George Harrison, and Ken Brown filled out the lineup.[14]

"Welcome to the Casbah," Lennon shouted before the opening number. "We are the Quarrymen and we are going to play you some rock and roll."[15] Their set included American rock-and-roll favorites such as Little Richard's "Long Tall Sally" and Chuck Berry's "Roll over Beethoven." Mona Best was sufficiently impressed with the four guitarists to offer them a regular weekly engagement at the Casbah. Their compensation was to be three pounds in cash and all the Cokes and bags of crisps (potato chips) the boys could consume.[16] This was an inauspicious beginning for what would become the most successful and influential band in history, but, as Paul McCartney later said, the Casbah "was the place where all that started."[17]

The Quarrymen's run at the Casbah lasted seven weeks, until a spat erupted one night over Mona's decision to give Ken Brown his share of the three pounds, even though he had stayed upstairs, sick with the flu. John, Paul, and George were furious and stormed out of the club. "Right, that's it, then," Paul shouted on the way out the door.[18]

By the time John, Paul, and George ended their boycott of the Casbah, their band would be called the Beatles, and Mona Best's son Pete would be the band's drummer. Mona welcomed the Beatles—John, Paul, George, and Pete—back to the Casbah in 1960, fresh off a successful extended booking in Hamburg, Germany. John, Paul, and George had become friendly with Pete (who, like his mother, had been born in India to English parents) during their early shows at the Casbah in 1959. The following year, Pete became the band's first regular drummer. By that time, the band had dropped Ken Brown and added Stuart Sutcliffe, an art school friend of John's who sold a painting for sixty pounds and was persuaded to buy an electric bass with the proceeds.[19] Stuart possessed only marginal musical talent and left the band in 1961, at which time McCartney took over on bass. Pete played with the Beatles for two years, including the band's three formative stints in Hamburg.

Situated on the Elbe River, Hamburg was (and remains) Germany's second-largest city and its primary port. But the Beatles spent the great majority of their time in Hamburg's infamous St. Pauli section, a red-light district filled with brothels, beer halls, and strip clubs. The band famously played marathon sets in seedy beer halls, honing their sound and freely indulging in sex, booze, and drugs. During their first stint in Hamburg, the Beatles slept in some extra rooms behind the screen of a sleazy movie theater. "We lived backstage in the Bambi-Kino, next to the toilets, and you could always smell them," McCartney recalled. "The room had been an old storeroom and there were just concrete walls and nothing else. No heat, no wallpaper, not a lick of paint, and some camp beds with not many sheets. We were frozen."[20]

In a varied string of music clubs named the Indira, the Kaiserkeller, the Star-Club, and the Top Ten, the Beatles played to eclectic and often rough crowds that included plenty of sailors and prostitutes, as well as businessmen, students, and tourists. As Lennon later explained, "We were born in Liverpool, but grew up in Hamburg."[21] They played long sets filled with songs recorded by American rock-and-roll pioneers. Sets lasting up to seven hours were standard on weeknights; they were even longer on weekends.[22] McCartney later recalled, "Our role in Hamburg was to make people buy more beer."[23] Given their long hours onstage during three extended stays in Germany's "sin city," Pete Best may well have spent more time onstage as the Beatles' drummer than Ringo Starr did, especially in light of the group's famous decision to cease touring in 1966.[24]

It was in Hamburg that the Beatles developed a devoted following and a musical chemistry that helped them land a recording audition at EMI's London studios on Abbey Road on June 6, 1962. Fresh off their third extended stay in Germany, John, Paul, George, and Pete recorded four tracks, including versions of the Lennon-McCartney original "Love Me Do" and a cover version of "Besame Mucho"—the only recordings from that fateful session known to have survived.[25]

Producer George Martin was not overly impressed with the band's songwriting capabilities and found the drumming to be lacking.[26] Martin told their manager, Brian Epstein, that the group would need to use a different drummer for future recordings. It was not uncommon in those days to use session musicians in the studio who were not part of the touring band—the Beatles themselves would help make the idea of bands writing their own music and playing their own instruments the norm.

On June 24, 1962, John, Paul, George, and Pete would play closing night at the Casbah Club, which Mona Best had decided to shut down after nearly three years of entertaining Liverpool's youth. Less than two months later, in August 1962, Pete Best was unceremoniously sacked after two years as the Beatles' drummer. Manager Brian Epstein was given the unenviable task of breaking the news to Pete. "We were cowards," Lennon would later recall. "We got Epstein to do the dirty work for us."[27] Epstein told Best, "The boys want you out and Ringo in. They don't think you're a good enough drummer, Pete. And George Martin doesn't think you're a good enough drummer."[28]

Martin's suggestion (or demand) that the Beatles use a hired drummer for recording sessions did not mean they had to replace Best. They still could have toured with Pete, and no one would have been the wiser. But Best was something of an odd man out by temperament and by virtue of being the last member to join the band. Further, Pete's mother, Mona, had been exerting a heavy influence over the band. This had been understandable when the lads were using her home as a clubhouse, but as they moved closer toward the brink of stardom, her input became less welcome.

In addition to winning the hearts of many female fans, Pete gained a reputation for being cool and aloof. He did not share the same penchant for clever banter that would endear the band to the press and the public. Best's mother believed the others in the group were jealous of Pete's good looks and his rapport with female fans. But even if jealousy did play some role, the simpler explanation for Pete's sacking is that someone in a position of power and authority in the recording industry had given the drummer a vote of no confidence, and his bandmates believed that he was expendable.[29] When the news of Pete's ouster broke, outraged fans staged protests in Liverpool, to no avail. Ringo was in, and there was no turning back for the Beatles.

Any band that included three songwriters with the talents of Lennon, McCartney, and Harrison would likely succeed, regardless of who played the drums. But there is an intangible element to a group of musicians, in addition to the sum of its parts. The Beatles—John, Paul, George, and Ringo—had that "chemistry," if any group ever did. Perhaps the Beatles would have succeeded with Pete Best on drums. Perhaps they would not have succeeded without Pete and Mona's contributions during the band's formative years. But Mona Best and her son Pete were indisputably significant players in the early years of the most successful and significant rock-and-roll band of the twentieth century—one that revolutionized and forever altered popular music.

Unabashedly influenced and inspired by early American rock acts such as Elvis Presley, Little Richard, Chuck Berry, and Buddy Holly, the Beatles would make an indelible mark on American music and culture. The music that formed the foundation of the Beatles' sound appeared in the aftermath of World War II, from which the United States emerged as the lone economic and cultural hegemon in the Western world. Though its deeper roots can be traced to Africa and Europe, rock and roll is quintessentially American, an amalgam of a variety of American musical genres, including blues, country, jazz, rhythm and blues, and gospel. Beginning with their groundbreaking appearance on *The Ed Sullivan Show* in February 1964—which generated what was, at the time, the largest audience for a commercially televised event—the Beatles led what would be called a "British invasion" of the American popular music scene that included such hit makers as the Rolling Stones, the Animals, Donovan, the Kinks, Herman's Hermits, and the Dave Clark Five.

Whereas the Beatles were four British lads who transformed American culture with music that was heavily influenced by American recording artists, Never Say Die was an American-born horse with a pedigree dominated by European influence that won England's greatest horse race. Although Never Say Die's Derby victory did not have the immediate impact on the sport of Thoroughbred racing that the Beatles had on Western culture, his win was an important sign of changes that had been taking place for decades. Vast fortunes with roots in the American industrial expansion of the late nineteenth and early twentieth centuries had made it possible for wealthy Americans and their heirs to purchase many of Europe's top Thoroughbreds from their aristocratic owners and import them to America for breeding purposes. By the 1960s and 1970s, American racehorses produced from those European bloodlines would be winning Europe's top races with regularity, and with lasting ramifications for the global Thoroughbred industry.

Chapter 2

The Unusual Origins of a Sewing Machine Fortune

Robert Sterling Clark could afford to breed and race Thoroughbreds at the world's highest levels because of his immense inherited fortune. That fortune had its roots in the Singer Manufacturing Company, which had introduced the sewing machine to the far reaches of the globe and revolutionized international commerce during the late-nineteenth-century industrial boom that followed the American Civil War. The remarkable success of the Singer brand was due in large part to Clark's grandfather, Edward Clark, whose vision and leadership made the company the first prosperous American multinational corporation. While it was the discipline and business acumen of Edward Clark that facilitated the astounding success of Singer Manufacturing, it was Clark's partner, the eccentric bigamist Isaac Merritt Singer, who was responsible for the technological innovations that gave rise to the first Singer sewing machine.

The partners' circuitous path to fabulous riches could hardly be called typical, but the story of the rise of Singer Manufacturing reveals much about the economic, social, and political atmosphere in late-nineteenth-century America that produced so many millionaires. Many of these nineteenth-century industrial tycoons and captains of finance would become major players in

American horse racing and breeding and would help establish the United States—and Kentucky in particular—as the center of an increasingly globalized Thoroughbred industry by the end of the twentieth century.

Isaac Singer, the youngest son of a German immigrant father and a Quaker mother, was born near Albany, New York, in 1811. Soon after Isaac's birth, his family moved west to Oswego, a village on the shores of Lake Ontario, where Singer's father found labor-intensive work in various capacities. Singer's parents divorced when he was ten, at a time when the only legal cause for divorce was adultery. His mother, who appears to have been the guilty party, returned to Albany and settled in a Quaker community, while his father quickly remarried. Isaac did not get along with his new stepmother and found life in her house unbearable.[1]

He left home at the age of twelve and headed to Rochester, a boomtown on the Erie Canal. That engineering marvel connecting the Great Lakes to the Eastern Seaboard indelibly altered the American economy and transformed society as it ushered in a great wave of westward migration and made New York City the nation's leading port and commercial center. All sorts of hangers-on and profiteers accompanied the thousands of laborers who worked on the canal beginning in 1817, including prostitutes, preachers, whiskey merchants, and gamblers. Eventually, the marks of modern civilization would come as well, including schools, newspapers, theaters, hotels, and churches. These trappings of modernity created a relatively cosmopolitan atmosphere in Rochester, an area that had been wilderness only a few years earlier.

Singer would stay in Rochester for seven years, living with grown siblings while working in the summers and acquiring a rudimentary education in the winters. In 1830 he decided it was time to learn a trade, so he indulged an interest in mechanical things and took an apprenticeship at a local machinist's shop. Meanwhile, he was moonlighting as an actor. Following a lo-

Isaac Merritt Singer, a failed actor and the father of at least two dozen children, created the Singer sewing machine, which became a worldwide best seller and earned him and company co-owner Edward Clark a sizable fortune. Isaac Merritt Singer, oil on canvas, by Edward Harrison May (1824–1887).

cal performance by a traveling theater troupe, Singer had approached the director and asked if he could join. He impressed the director with his knowledge of Shakespeare and landed the lead role in *Richard III*. The local crowds were thrilled with his performance, particularly with the famous line "A horse, a horse, my kingdom for a horse!"[2]

Singer hit the road with the troupe but found the crowds much less responsive than his hometown audience, and soon there were no more parts for him. He took contract work as a machinist in Auburn, New York, sixty miles east of Rochester, beginning a pattern of alternating between periods of itinerant labor and stints with theater companies in various capacities. At the end of the year he married a fifteen-year-old girl named Catharine Marie Haley from a small town outside Rochester. Singer continued to take acting jobs when he could find them and odd jobs when he could not.

The United States in the first half of the nineteenth century was a nation on the move as white settlers continued to press west. As the frontier moved farther and farther inland, a national market economy was developing, and innovations in technology and transportation revolutionized the way people lived. Isaac Singer was well suited for that environment, as he was not one to let the dust settle beneath him. Soon after Catharine and Isaac's first child was born in 1834, the family moved to New York City, where Isaac took a job in a press shop. But before long he was back on the road, this time as an agent for a theatrical company, leaving Catharine and their young son behind.

At one of the company's performances during a protracted engagement in Baltimore, an eighteen-year-old audience member named Mary Ann Sponsler caught Singer's eye. After the show was over, Singer sought out the brown-haired, blue-eyed beauty and managed to coax from her an invitation to her parents' house. He quickly became a friend of the family and took up residence at the Sponsler home for the duration of his stay in Baltimore.

Unaware that Singer was already married, Mary Ann's parents—the proprietor of a local oyster cannery and his wife—encouraged the tall, well-traveled theater man in what they believed to be an honest and legitimate desire to court their daughter. Soon Singer and Mary Ann were engaged. But there was the problem of his wife in New York.[3]

Singer asked Mary Ann to wait for him in Baltimore while he attended to some "business" in New York, where, between mutual accusations of infidelities, he and Catharine managed to conceive another child before agreeing to a separation. Catharine gave birth to their daughter the following year before leaving New York City to live with her parents in the western part of the state. In the meantime, Mary Ann made good on her promise to join Isaac in New York, but he was less accommodating in making good on his promise to marry her. Singer explained that there was a problem: another woman believed she was his wife, which made marriage a tricky proposition for the moment. Mary Ann reluctantly agreed to live with Isaac as his wife until he could get the other situation straightened out, and the following summer the couple's first child was born.[4]

Within weeks of the birth, Singer was ready to hit the road on another theater tour. Mary Ann was not happy with the prospect of caring for a newborn alone, so she returned to Baltimore with their son. For the next two years, Isaac knocked around the Midwest before landing in Chicago, where he got a job working for his brother on the construction of the Illinois and Michigan Canal, which would eventually connect Lake Michigan with the Gulf of Mexico via the Illinois and Mississippi Rivers, making Chicago a major commercial transportation hub. While working on the canal, Singer invented a horse-powered rock drill that facilitated the labor-intensive excavation process. He sold the patent for $2,000, which was a serious amount of money at that time.

Singer chose to plow those proceeds straight into the creation of his own theater company, which he would call the Merritt

Players (Isaac Merritt being his stage name). He then convinced Mary Ann, his pseudo-wife, to join him in Chicago as an actress in the company. For the next few years, the small outfit bounced from town to town, performing Shakespeare and temperance dramas (a popular form of theater at the time that preached—usually to the converted—about the ills of alcohol abuse). The Merritt Players had difficulty drawing audiences, however, and eventually the company was reduced to Isaac and Mary Ann traveling in a two-horse wagon with their brood, which by then numbered four children.

When the curtain finally closed on the Merritt Players for the last time, the Singers were in Fredericksburg, Ohio, where Isaac found work in a print shop, assisting in the production of posters and advertisements. Singer was assigned to create typeface from wooden blocks, and again his ingenuity kicked into action. He began to work on a machine that could carve typefaces out of metal and wood. Two years later, Singer and his family moved to Pittsburgh, where Isaac set up shop as a printer. He continued to experiment with his carving machine while operating his printing and sign-making business until 1849, when he returned to New York City in hopes of cashing in on his invention. Singer and the family—now consisting of eight children—settled in the Lower East Side, not far from where Catharine Haley (still legally married to Singer) and her two children were living. Catharine had recently returned to Manhattan after an extended stay with her parents.

Singer was optimistic about his family's chances to thrive in New York, but his plans to cash in on his printing invention suffered a major setback in the form of a deadly boiler explosion at the Hague Street manufacturing building where Singer's prototype was stored. Sixty-three people were killed and dozens more injured in one of the worst industrial disasters anyone could remember. Singer was not in the building at the time of the explosion, but his machine was completely destroyed. Fortunately, a bookseller and former publisher named George B. Zieber had seen Isaac's machine before its demise and believed that he could market it to publishing houses. In 1850 Singer and Zieber secured space on the ground floor of a machine shop owned by Orson C. Phelps in Boston—the heart of the American publishing industry. There the pair reconstructed Singer's typeface-carving machine. Although people came to see Singer's invention, no one showed much interest in buying it.[5]

Meanwhile, on the second floor of the building, workers were busy manufacturing a sewing machine created by a pair of innovators; it was a modified version of a machine patented only three years earlier by Elias Howe.[6] The manufacturers were having trouble with their product, which was unreliable and difficult to operate. Phelps asked Singer to take a look at the sewing machine upstairs to see if he could apply his creativity to improve the product. At first reluctant to turn his attention away from his own machine, which he felt had a much greater potential for profit than any sewing contraption, Singer quickly drafted a sketch for an improved design that met with Phelps's enthusiastic approval. Zieber drafted a contract, and Singer, Phelps, and Zieber entered into a partnership to manufacture sewing machines.[7]

Within two weeks they had constructed a working model that incorporated a vertically moving needle suspended from an overhanging arm that sewed material situated on a horizontal plane, powered by a foot pedal.[8] Isaac Singer did not invent the sewing machine, and he never claimed to have done so. But he and his partners were very enthusiastic about their product; unlike earlier models, it was practical and reliable and could produce 900 stitches per minute. There were some significant obstacles to overcome, however, before their enthusiasm could be turned into profit. Not the least of these was the fact that there was no perceived need for sewing machines in the American marketplace.

Labor was cheap in the mid-nineteenth-century industrial Northeast. Sewing was one of the few jobs available to women on a large scale at that time, and clothes makers were not interested in expensive machinery, no matter how many stitches per minute were promised, particularly given early models' reputation for unreliability. To combat these negative perceptions, Singer took his model on tour, setting up outside circuses, carnivals, or wherever crowds gathered, to demonstrate the simplicity and capabilities of his machine. He also employed diminutive women and set them up in attractively decorated showroom windows to verify the ease with which even "non-mechanically inclined" females could operate a sewing machine.[9]

In the operation's early days, the partners struggled to survive financially, which might explain Orson Phelps's willingness to sell his interest in the company for $1,000 down and $3,000 to be paid in installments, along with an agreement that the machines would continue to be manufactured in Phelps's shop. Additionally, Phelps allowed himself to be talked into working as a traveling sales agent for Singer.[10]

Another early problem for the Singer group was the fact that the machine incorporated innovations that had been patented by others, including inventor Elias Howe. Howe spotted a Singer machine in a fancy showroom window, recognized that it used some of his patents, and offered Singer the exclusive right to manufacture under his patents in exchange for $2,000. Had Singer accepted Howe's deal, he might have saved the company millions in the long run, but the money simply was not available, and the offer had to be refused. Instead, seeing the likelihood of lawsuits on the horizon, Singer sought the help of New York City lawyer Edward Clark (Robert Sterling Clark's grandfather) and offered him a one-third interest in the company (which would then be known as I. M. Singer and Company) in exchange for his legal assistance. Singer had previously enlisted Clark, a junior partner in the successful firm Jordan, Clark, and Company, to help settle some issues surrounding ownership and patent rights connected to Singer's typeface-carving machine. In those dealings, Clark had accepted a percentage of ownership in the carving machine in lieu of payment. Little came of Clark's involvement with that invention, but his decision to join the sewing machine business would have global ramifications.[11]

Singer and Clark, who had been born only three months and some fifty miles apart, could scarcely have been more different. Clark's father had founded Athens Pottery Works a few years before Edward's birth, and it soon became nationally known and enjoyed a virtual monopoly in the upstate New York market. His father's success afforded Edward the opportunity to be educated at a Massachusetts boarding school before enrolling at Williams College, where he would be among its first graduates in 1831. Upon graduation from Williams, Clark read law under Ambrose L. Jordan in Hudson, New York. After a three-year apprenticeship with Jordan, Clark was admitted to the New York bar and set up a private practice in Poughkeepsie. He married Jordan's daughter and eventually established a practice with his father-in-law in New York City. Jordan's high profile in New York State politics helped the firm quickly become one of the city's most prestigious. Clark's quiet demeanor and status as a Sunday school teacher belied his steely nerve and business sense. By the time of his death in 1882, Clark would be worth more than $50 million, a formidable fortune in nineteenth-century America.

After adding Clark as a partner, Singer would soon be looking to divest himself of another partner. George B. Zieber had approached Clark just before the lawyer officially joined the operation to express his frustration with what he felt was Singer's mistreatment of him. Business was not yet booming, and Clark recognized that Zieber might be willing to sell his stake in the company. An opportunity to part Zieber from that stake presented itself when he became bedridden with what turned out to be a relatively minor illness. According to Zieber, Singer visited him in his sickbed with a report, ostensibly from Zieber's doctor, that he was not likely to survive his ailment. Armed with this information and a desire to pay some outstanding debts before he died, Zieber agreed to sell his portion of the company to Singer and Clark for $6,000. With Singer's ingenuity and Clark's organizational and business sense, the pair made a formidable team. Their next task would be to deal with the bevy of lawsuits that were being initiated against Singer and the company for patent infringement.[12]

In 1854 Clark settled Elias Howe's claim against their company with an agreement to pay a $25 royalty on all machines sold until the expiration of Howe's patent, an arrangement that would net Howe as much as $2 million over the next thirteen years. Then, in 1856, the major holders of sewing machine patents, including Howe and Singer, met in Albany, New York, and formed a patent pool, the first of its kind in America. The pool allowed members to use patents held by other members without legal repercussions. With an agreement in place that would survive until the last patent expired in 1877, the members of the Sewing Machine Combination could devote more time to sales and less to litigation.[13]

Freed from the burden of pending litigation, Singer and Clark prospered. Singer was a fearless self-promoter. Utilizing skills sharpened by time spent onstage and in promoting the theater, Singer marketed himself as a "self-made man"—a moniker that was fashionable at the time—and traveled the East Coast demonstrating the wonders of the sewing machine to anyone who would watch. He even enlisted some of his teenaged sons to do likewise. His product was indeed an improvement on what had existed before, but, without Singer's marketing skills and tireless promotional energy, the company likely would not have survived long enough to demonstrate the superiority of its machines.

Using interchangeable parts, a technique first employed in America in the manufacture of muskets for the War of 1812, Singer drastically reduced the time and cost of production. In addition to being innovators on the production side, Singer and

Clark worked to broaden the market for sewing machines to include households as well as factories.[14] Soon after the creation of the Sewing Machine Combination, Singer introduced his first machine designed for use in the home, which he dubbed the "turtle back." But at $125, the cost was prohibitive; the average household income was only around $500 per year. To lure customers, Clark hatched a rent-to-own program in which buyers could put as little as $5 down and pay $5 per month—a revolutionary scheme at the time. The pair also offered to pay $50 for a "trade-in" of any model of sewing machine, which they promised to immediately destroy. They were very much on the cutting edge when it came to marketing and financing techniques, many of which have survived into the twenty-first century.[15] The success of the "turtle back" drove annual Singer sales from 2,500 sewing machines in 1856 to 13,000 only four years later.

One key to Singer and Clark's domestic success was their ability to tap into the growing middle-class market. A barrier to that market was the need to convince the breadwinning men of those households that it was in their interest to pay a relatively large amount of money for a device that would only save their wives time and effort. There was also the issue of whether it was "ladylike" for a Victorian middle-class woman to be operating machinery in her living room (or whether it was even *possible* for women to operate such "complicated" machinery). These issues were not as important to the lower classes, as there were tremendous profits to be made by women willing to farm out their sewing services to clothing manufacturers, but the cost of the machines was prohibitive. Additionally, there was the broader concern that the widespread implementation of machines would put people out of work and lead to devastating poverty and starvation. To combat all these concerns in one fell swoop, Clark initiated a plan to offer sewing machines to ministers' wives for half the standard retail price.[16] By using the pious ladies as unwitting marketing assistants, he showed that Singer machines were socially and morally acceptable and easy for women to operate.[17]

But just as Clark's efforts to create a middle-class-friendly image for Singer machines were beginning to take hold, big trouble loomed. Clark was forced to turn his attention to the scandalous mess that Isaac Singer had made of his personal life, which the *New York Herald* called "A Very Ghastly Domestic Story" and which threatened to wipe out all of Clark's progress in creating a positive image for their company and product.[18]

In January 1860 Isaac Singer and his first wife, Catharine Haley (who had been leading a quiet life with another man on Long Island while still legally married to Singer), finally divorced. Because of Clark's concern that Singer's unusual domestic situation could have a detrimental effect on the company, which prided itself on having a "wholesome" image, someone from the Singer camp had contacted Catharine's lawyer and offered her $10,000 to divorce Singer. Catharine had been receiving financial support from Singer for years, but the divorce offer included a vague suggestion that the sewing machine company's financial prospects were uncertain, with the implicit recommendation that she would do well to agree to the terms while there was still any money to be had (in reality, the company was in fine shape). Believing that Singer's maintenance payments might dry up, Catharine accepted the $10,000, and the couple obtained a divorce on the grounds of Catharine's "adultery" with her lover, a face-saving maneuver for Singer and the company.[19]

Mary Ann, with whom Singer had been living in a de facto marriage for nearly twenty-five years, assumed that after Singer's divorce from Haley, he would finally marry her. She was very much mistaken, however; Singer had no intention of ever marrying Mary Ann, despite the fact that she had borne him ten children and the couple lived together in their lavish home at 14 Fifth Avenue. They enjoyed all the material trappings of the era, including Singer's canary yellow nine-horse carriage—called a "steamboat on wheels" by a local newspaper—which included space for thirty-one passengers, a security team, a band, and a nursery.[20] If Mary Ann was disappointed by Singer's (latest) refusal to marry her, a chance discovery a few months later would leave her downright despondent and would eventually lead to the unraveling of Singer's astonishing web of deceit.

In August 1860 Mary Ann was driving her carriage down Fifth Avenue when she passed Singer traveling in the opposite direction in an open carriage accompanied by Mary McGonigal, confirming hushed rumors of the untoward nature of their association. At the sight of her ersatz husband joyriding with another woman, Mary Ann let out a blood-curdling scream, heard by Singer and hundreds of passersby. Overcome with emotion, Mary Ann quickly made her way back to the couple's home, where Singer met her. Enraged at the public spectacle she had made, Singer beat Sponsler severely and then choked her into unconsciousness. Singer was later arrested on charges of assault, and scarcely a month later he was aboard a ship bound for England.[21]

The situation became even more outrageous when it was revealed that McGonigal had borne Singer five children. He had been supporting that family in a house on Christopher Street, where McGonigal and Singer were known as Mr. and Mrs. Mathews. Additionally, it was soon discovered that Singer had fathered a daughter with another woman—Mary Eastwood Walters, who was living on West Twenty-seventh Street (supported by Singer) as Mrs. Merritt.[22]

The fact that Singer had been supporting three families in addition to his legally recognized one infuriated the conservative Clark. It would take all his skills of negotiation and persuasion to fix the mess that Singer had made of his personal life. Fortunately for the company, the Civil War pushed the sordid details of the ensuing court battles to the back pages of the city's many newspapers. Realizing that her and her children's claim to Singer's wealth might be no stronger than that of any number of other women, Mary Ann Sponsler quickly filed for divorce from Singer, claiming that she had been his common-law wife for the seven months the two had lived together after his divorce from Catharine. A judge granted her petition and awarded her a then-record $8,000 per year in alimony. But before the order could be executed, Mary Ann agreed to accept a comfortable Manhattan house and $50 a month instead.

In the wake of these complicated proceedings, Clark became further convinced that he had to distance both himself and the firm (which he had built into an international cash cow) from Singer. Details of Singer's personal life were making their way into various court documents and newspaper pages, and they were hardly in step with the corporate image Clark had worked so hard to create. Singer's opulent lifestyle was only working to drain the firm of resources, and Clark was concerned that additional claimants on Singer's wealth might emerge. So in 1863, he convinced Singer to agree to dissolve the partnership. The two replaced it with a joint-stock company called Singer Manufacturing Company. Clark wanted to ensure that Singer had no direct control over the company and agreed to limit his own involvement to achieve that end. Clark and Singer agreed that neither would serve as president of the company as long as the other man was alive, and a former Singer clerk named Inslee Hopper was appointed the company's first president.[23]

Clark remained actively involved in the company, and during the Civil War he managed to metaphorically drape the Singer product in the American flag by donating 1,000 machines to the Union Army, employing the marketing slogan "We Clothe the Union Armies—While Grant Is Dressing the Rebels."[24] The need for soldiers' uniforms fueled a demand for sewing machines, and Clark's strategy of making their product a patriotic one only helped Singer's position in the market. By that time, factories and sales offices across the United States were selling 21,000 sewing machines annually.

Clark's commercial innovations helped Singer Manufacturing Company steadily increase its American market share. The names of rival companies, such as Grover and Baker and Wheeler and Wilson, would soon be forgotten by history, and Singer would eventually achieve a virtual monopoly in the sewing machine market. But it was on the international stage that Singer truly began to blossom as the first successful American multinational corporation. Its international sales had helped the company survive the American depression of 1857, and by the end of the Civil War, it had sold more machines abroad than in the United States, eventually accessing markets around the globe and distributing instruction manuals in fifty languages.

The Singer product was so successful and ubiquitous that the name *Singer* became synonymous with *sewing machine* in many places, a linguistic connection that proved difficult for competitors to sever. An article appearing in the *Chicago Tribune* predicted that "the future historian, in reviewing the progress of civilization, will make the perfection of the sewing-machine the beginning of a new era," and it credited Singer as being "first and foremost among the clear-headed and ingenious men who bridged the gaps of imperfection."[25] By 1870, Singer was producing over 125,000 units annually, a number that would grow to 600,000 by the 1880s.[26]

A week after formally dissolving the partnership and effectively being ousted from daily involvement with the company he had founded, Singer married a pregnant European divorcée named Isabella Boyer in New York. He eventually had six children with her, and after being shunned by "society" in New York and Yonkers (where Singer built a gargantuan home he called "The Castle"), the couple moved permanently to Europe. They first settled in Paris but abandoned the City of Lights during the Franco-Prussian War and moved to an English seaside estate in Devon, where Singer's acreage included some twenty cottages and build-

ings. There, Singer built a 115-room mansion named "Oldway," fit for a lord and complete with gardens, conservatories, a covered riding arena, and an in-house theater.[27]

The couple was never completely accepted by British aristocrats, but local townsfolk eventually welcomed them. Two thousand locals witnessed Isaac Merritt Singer's funeral procession in 1875, which stretched nearly a mile long and consisted of some seventy carriages. Singer left a sizable estate estimated to be worth $13 million, which gave rise to a number of lawsuits involving several of his two dozen children and various ex-"wives." The following year Edward Clark replaced Inslee Hopper as company president, a title he would retain until his own death.[28]

With the expiration of most major sewing machine patents on the horizon, Clark slashed the price of Singer's best-selling model to $30 in 1877, ensuring a broad and loyal customer base when the market became flooded with imitations soon thereafter. He also set a policy of investing the company's surplus revenues in conservative securities that would allow Singer Manufacturing to ride out panics, depressions, and world wars in the com-

Oldway Mansion exterior and interior. Rejected by New York society, Isaac Merritt Singer commissioned the construction of this lavish home in Devon, England, in 1871. The residence was not completed until shortly after Singer's death in 1875. It was remodeled in the early 1900s at the direction of Singer's son, Paris. (Ianmacm at en.wikipedia)

Edward Clark financed the construction of the Dakota (shown here in 1890), which was completed two years after his death, in 1884. In 1980 the building gained international notoriety as the site of John Lennon's murder. (Library of Congress, Prints and Photographs Division, NY-5467)

ing decades. Clark showed similar foresight in the handling of his own wealth. In 1880 he began construction on the Dakota, a luxury apartment building located in what was then the outskirts of Manhattan, at West Seventy-second Street.[29] The building's name would become seared in the minds of music fans across the world as the site of John Lennon's murder 100 years later.

But Edward Clark would not live to see the Dakota completed. He died in 1882, after catching pneumonia on a night boat on the Hudson traveling from New York City to Cooperstown, where he spent much of his leisure time after building a mansion called "Fernleigh" there. In addition to an estate estimated to be worth $50 million, Clark could claim the Singer Manufacturing Company as his legacy. His leadership and vision were primarily responsible for the firm's unprecedented worldwide success. Clark's heirs would reap the benefits of his work at

Singer, maintaining a controlling interest in the company for the next seventy-seven years.[30]

Clark's wife and three of his four children had preceded him in death. His only surviving son and sole heir to a serious fortune, Alfred Corning Clark, was a kind and generous man who lived something of a double life. In New York he was a respected businessman, husband, father, and philanthropist. But he also spent a considerable amount of time in Europe, where he was a patron of the arts and music and maintained a semicloseted but thoroughly committed homosexual relationship. Before his death, Edward Clark had been concerned about the amount of time Alfred was spending in Europe, so Edward decided to leave his vast real estate holdings to his four grandchildren—Alfred's four sons. When Alfred himself died at the age of fifty-one in 1896, he also left his sons an enormous monetary fortune, as well as a passion for sports and European culture. Alfred's second son, Robert Sterling Clark, would combine the elements of his inheritance into one of the finest collections of European paintings in the world and a world-class stable of Thoroughbreds.

Chapter 3

Robert Sterling Clark

In addition to reaching the very apex of the sport of Thoroughbred racing with Never Say Die's Epsom Derby win in 1954, Robert Sterling Clark would travel the world, build one of the finest collections of Impressionist paintings, battle his siblings in a high-profile inheritance dispute, and be accused of involvement in a plot to overthrow President Franklin D. Roosevelt. But with the possible exception of the art museum he built in Williamstown, Massachusetts, Clark's most lasting legacy would be his victory in the Epsom Derby and the example he set for future globe-trotting horsemen. Clark showed the world that it was possible for an American horse to win at Europe's highest levels at a time when American racehorses were still widely believed to be vastly inferior to European runners.

Born in 1877, Clark was the second son of Alfred Corning Clark and Elizabeth Scriven Clark. During childhood he split time between his family's New York City residences and the Fernleigh mansion in Cooperstown, where the Clarks spent summers in an idyllic setting amid lakes, streams, and meadows. It was in Cooperstown that Sterling, as his friends called him, developed a love for horses and riding. He studied engineering at Yale and, after graduation, joined the army.

Clark participated in the invasion of the Philippines during

Robert Sterling Clark's love of horses began at an early age. He is pictured here at his family's Cooperstown, New York, estate, circa 1890. (© Sterling and Francine Clark Art Institute, Williamstown, Massachusetts)

the Spanish-American War and in the suppression of the Boxer Rebellion, a populist Chinese uprising that opposed a Western imperialist presence in China. These American military operations were part of a growing U.S. commitment to join the European competition for overseas empire and spheres of economic influence that would guarantee markets for American goods and secure a place for the United States among the ranks of world superpowers. In one sense, the United States' decision to enter the race for empire represented a dramatic shift in policy for a nation that had never attempted to win territory through overseas war before. But in another sense, Americans had been pushing west since the first Europeans settled in the New World. Americans had steadily expanded their territory since the colonial era, reached the Pacific Ocean in the mid-nineteenth century, and simply kept going.[1]

By the early twentieth century, the ever-expanding Ameri-

Robert Sterling Clark, the "Millionaire Lieutenant," circa 1900. He served with the U.S. Army in the Philippines during the Spanish-American War and in China during the Boxer Rebellion.

can industrial economy had become inextricably entangled with diplomatic and military policy. This marriage of industry and diplomacy worked to the great benefit of American businessmen and financiers, many of whom would become heavily involved in horse racing and breeding. The scions and heirs of these early industrialists, including Robert Sterling Clark, would make the American Thoroughbred industry the strongest in the world by the end of the century.

Upon returning to the States following his military service, Sterling took a position with the Department of War in Washington, where he enjoyed a busy social life and was known as the "millionaire lieutenant." But the romance of adventure in far-off places beckoned, and in 1905 Sterling traveled to England and then to India, where he began preparations for a major research expedition through northern China to study and document the geology, topography, flora, fauna, monasteries, and monuments of the region.

In preparation for the journey that he would finance himself, Sterling assembled a team that included a doctor, a meteorologist, an artist, an interpreter, a naturalist, a surveyor, fifteen muleteers, eight personal servants, two surveyors, eight ponies, forty-four mules, five donkeys, and two grooms. Despite diligent preparation, the planned eighteen-month, 2,000-mile trek was cut short when a surveyor was murdered under mysterious circumstances. Before returning from the field, however, the team managed to do some important work that Sterling would later publish.[2]

At the conclusion of his research, Sterling moved to Paris, where he bought a house on rue Cimarosa, near the Arc de Triomphe. He turned his attention to furnishing and decorating his spacious three-story dwelling and coauthoring an account of his Chinese adventure, which would be published in 1912. It was during this period that Sterling began to develop two interests that would envelop much of the rest of his life: collecting art and arguing with his siblings.

Sterling had been in Asia when his younger brother Stephen, an attorney in New York, had undertaken the task of dividing their parents' furniture and paintings among the four brothers. Sterling felt that he had been shortchanged in the process and was especially perturbed by his brother's suggestion that Sterling might wish to purchase some of the pieces Stephen had kept for himself. Stephen's letter offering the paintings for sale referred to "my mother" and was coldly signed "very sincerely yours, Stephen C. Clark."[3] Sterling had previously shown no special interest in artwork, but he had a new Parisian house to decorate and idle hours to devote to such pursuits. Thus, the issue took on heightened importance. Further, as the Clark brothers were coming into full adulthood, the paintings could be seen as representative of a competition for the status and power their father and grandfather had wielded.

Though the brothers managed to make amends after this initial squabble, it was a predictor of more serious disagreements to come and the beginning of an art-collecting competition that would last the rest of their lives. Sterling soon became completely absorbed in the acquisition of paintings and developed a particular taste for the works of Pierre-Auguste Renoir. Sterling pursued masterpieces with the same determination and passion he had shown in the organization of his Chinese expedition and would later show in the development of his stable of racehorses.

Sterling's pursuit of the paintings of the European masters was put on hold in 1917 when he joined the French World War I effort as a liaison to the American military, serving in Paris and Bordeaux until 1919. Upon leaving the military again, Sterling finally married, at age forty-two, a French former actress named Francine Clary, with whom he had lived for the better part of a decade. For the more conservative among Clark's family, his decision to marry Clary came as something of a shock: she was mother to an illegitimate child, and she herself had been born to unwed parents of Polish Catholic ancestry.[4]

Though they kept the Parisian mansion, Francine and Sterling decided to take an eighteen-room apartment on Park Avenue in order to spend more time in his native New York City. But proximity bred contempt, and not long after Sterling's return to New York, tensions between Sterling and his brother Stephen returned. Stephen and his wife were concerned about Sterling's carefree spending habits, which included regular purchases of Impressionist paintings, rugs, vintage wine, and antiques. Under the terms of their inheritance trusts, as long as Sterling remained childless (his wife's child did not qualify), the bulk of Sterling's share of the family estate would pass to Stephen's children upon Sterling's death.

Robert Sterling Clark met former actress Francine Clary in Paris in 1910, and the two were married in 1919. The fact that she had a child from a previous relationship did not endear her to Clark's family, but the marriage lasted until Sterling's death in 1956. *Mr. and Mrs. Clark* (1967), by Paul Lewis Clemens (American, 1911–1992); oil on canvas, 19³/₁₆ by 14¼ inches. (Image 1967.84, © Sterling and Francine Clark Art Institute, Williamstown, Massachusetts; photo by Michael Agee)

With the subject of the family trusts brought to the forefront, Sterling became more conscious of the fact that his wife and stepdaughter were not recognized under the trusts' terms. He summoned his three brothers to a meeting at the office of their financial administrator to discuss the possibility of gaining more autonomy over their inheritance. At the meeting, Stephen and Sterling came to blows, and their fisticuffs left both men bloodied. Sterling left the meeting and soon withdrew all the funds he directly controlled from the accounts managed by the family's financial adviser. He then established an office on Wall Street from which he managed his own financial affairs.

Four years later, Sterling filed a lawsuit against the president of Singer Manufacturing, the trustees in charge of his trust, and his brothers. The terms of the trust made it clear that neither his wife nor her daughter could ever access the thousands of shares of Singer stock that was at the heart of the trust's value. At issue were dividends generated by the Singer stock, which Sterling had assigned to the trust years before. He claimed that when he had signed the document that pooled the dividends with the shares themselves, he was not aware that he could do otherwise. Sterling lost the suit and would never speak to his brothers again.[5]

Repeated attempts at reconciliation were rebuffed by Sterling. "May God curse them all for their double dealing with a trusting man like myself and may I see them suffer morally and materially," Sterling wrote in his diary. He held special venom for Stephen, whom he called "that swine and treacherous sneak."[6] Soon Sterling would turn that wrath toward the institution of the federal income tax and focus his attention on reducing his burden thereunder, but in the meantime, he busied himself with the acquisition of expensive paintings and Thoroughbreds.

Sterling's love of horses began at an early age during rides with his family in Cooperstown. His growing interest in Thoroughbred racing allowed him to indulge both his affection for horses and his affinity for expensive items and European culture. As with his other passions, once Sterling decided to embark on building a top-notch racing stable, he pursued that goal with great gusto. Sterling's first serious success on the racetrack came in 1928 with his filly named Current, who was the greatest two-year-old of her generation. Among her stakes wins that year was the Selima Stakes at Laurel Park outside Baltimore, named for an eighteenth-century mare whose sire was the Godolphin Arabian, one of three stallions to whom all Thoroughbreds can trace their lineage (the other two are the Darley Arabian and the Byerly Turk).[7] The mare Selima had been imported to the United States in the 1750s to Belair Stud in Maryland. Following Current's win in the Selima Stakes, the owner of Belair Stud, William Woodward, presented a trophy to the winner.[8]

Later, as chairman of the Jockey Club, Woodward would play a role in Clark's decision to race exclusively in Europe as a result of a dispute over the registration of some of Clark's horses. But for the time being, Sterling was becoming increasingly enamored of horse racing and of his racehorses in America. He found himself spending more and more time in Kentucky and realized that he could reduce his state income tax burden by establishing residency in the Bluegrass State. So in 1929 he bought Walnut Springs Farm outside Lexington and began to renovate the main house there with his typical focused determination.[9]

Central Kentucky had been known for its fertile, nutrient-rich soil since the days of Daniel Boone, but it did not cement its status as America's preeminent commercial breeding center until the late nineteenth and early twentieth centuries, when ownership of large Kentucky horse farms—complete with neo-Confederate mansions—was in vogue for wealthy eastern horsemen. At a time when American racing faced the possibility of extinction at the hands of "progressive" reform groups opposed to the gambling aspect of the sport, Kentucky was one of the few states where racing had survived unscathed. The emergence of the Kentucky Derby as America's most popular horse race in the early twentieth century only enhanced the state's reputation as "horse country." In acquiring Kentucky acreage for his equine stock, Clark was following in the footsteps of a number of wealthy horsemen from the Northeast, including Harry Payne Whitney, August Belmont II, and James R. Keene.

In 1930 Clark acquired a horse farm in Normandy, France, complete with a manor house and gardens on 120 acres outside the town of Livarot; soon thereafter he abandoned his Kentucky home. Clark's wife may not have been particularly fond of Kentucky and generally did not share Sterling's growing passion for horse racing. Nevertheless, in 1932 he bought a 46-acre farm in Upperville, Virginia (outside Washington, D.C.), which he called "Sundridge." He also registered his racing silks—"cerise and grey stripes, quarter cap, blue sash"—with British racing authorities so he could race in England.[10]

Sterling's Virginia farm was adjacent to Rokeby Farm, purchased by Andrew W. Mellon (in his son Paul's name) for his ex-wife Nora to live on after their divorce. The farm reminded Nora of the countryside of her native England and afforded her the opportunity to live the life of an English lady (she had imagined doing so when she married Mellon, but the realities of industrial Pittsburgh had failed to meet her romantic visions of America). Nora eventually grew tired of country living, but her son would later turn Rokeby into the home base of his powerful Rokeby Stables, in whose name Mellon's horses would win both the Kentucky and Epsom Derbies.[11]

Before he guided the U.S. Treasury through the Roaring Twenties as one of the most powerful secretaries of the treasury since Alexander Hamilton, Andrew Mellon had amassed a fortune worth hundreds of millions of dollars through banking, the Alcoa Corporation, Gulf Oil, and mining interests. In 1924 Senator Robert M. La Follette famously quipped, "Andrew W. Mellon today is the real President of the United States. Calvin Coolidge is merely the man who occupies the White House."[12] As an illustration of the magnitude of Mellon's wealth, in 1926 only Henry Ford and John D. Rockefeller paid more taxes than he did. Mellon was a leader in Pittsburgh business and political circles when that city was an industrial giant and home to some of the biggest corporations and wealthiest citizens in America. But the onset of the Great Depression spelled the end of Mellon's influential stint at the Treasury, which had spanned three presidencies. The tide of the Great Depression swept Franklin D. Roosevelt into office in 1933, to the chagrin of many wealthy Americans, including Robert Sterling Clark.

In 1934 Sterling's attention would turn away from more trivial matters like horse racing and art collecting when the *New York Times* released reports from the House Committee on Un-American Activities revealing a plot to overthrow President Roosevelt with a private army of 500,000 ex-soldiers; the coup was to be financed by a group of wealthy and concerned citizens that allegedly included Clark. General Smedley D. Butler, with whom Clark had served in China, testified that Clark's agent had offered him $18,000 to address the convention of the American Legion in Chicago regarding the need to return the dollar to the gold standard. At a subsequent face-to-face meeting, Butler testified, Clark told him that he was prepared to spend half his fortune to save the other half and that Butler could convince the ex-soldiers to join the cause. Other testimony before the House committee accused Clark of financing agents' trips to Europe to study veterans groups' success in ousting governments there. After hearing eight months of testimony that filled 4,300 pages, the committee concluded that the plot was indeed legitimate.[13]

Clark had conveniently been in Europe when called to testify himself. But he issued a statement published by *Time* magazine in which he admitted that he had attempted to persuade Butler "to use his influence with the [American Legion] against the dollar devaluation." But, Clark resolutely added, "I am neither a Fascist nor a Communist, but an American." He then threatened to sue for libel "unless the whole affair is relegated to the funny sheets by Sunday."[14] Fortunately for Clark and his legacy, news agencies did not take the accusations seriously at first and failed to pursue the story even when the House committee determined that the claims and allegations had some basis in reality. The matter was soon forgotten almost entirely in a nation whose burdens imposed by the Great Depression would be lifted only by the onset of World War II. In the meantime, Roosevelt managed to persevere amid challenges and criticism from both the political Right and Left, allowing American capitalism and democracy to survive their greatest threat since the Civil War.

With the plot forgotten, the only time Clark's name appeared in the newspaper was related to his exploits as the owner of top racehorses. In 1939 he made headlines at home and abroad when his filly Galatea II won a pair of English classics, the One Thousand Guineas and the English Oaks. Clark had always been interested in Europe and its culture, and racing at the highest levels there allowed him to be a part of European high society. But by the late 1930s, Sterling had added incentive to race in Europe. Earlier in the decade the Jockey Club, which controlled the registration of Thoroughbreds in the United States from its New York City headquarters, had refused to officially recognize some horses Clark had bred from Arabian mares. Clark took the decision personally and was particularly upset with Jockey Club chairman William Woodward (master of Belair Stud and the man who had presented a silver trophy to Clark following his filly's victory in the Selima Stakes more than a decade earlier). Clark vowed never to race in the United States again as a result of this perceived slight, and he would focus on English racing for the rest of his life.

Sterling's later triumph with Never Say Die in the Epsom Derby must have been all the sweeter knowing that one of Woodward's great (and unfulfilled) ambitions in life was to win the Derby. As Woodward's grandson would later recall, Woodward

William Woodward Sr. aspired to be the second American to win the Epsom Derby with an American-bred horse. But it was Robert Sterling Clark (with whom Woodward had a famous run-in while serving as president of the Jockey Club) who would earn that distinction. (Keeneland Library)

had "strong feelings that whatever was English was good, and he wanted to be a part of that. He was a total anglophile."[15] And Woodward himself admitted that, as a young boy, "[he] made up [his] mind to be the second American to win the Derby."[16] Woodward started a total of thirteen horses in the Epsom Derby, but Sterling Clark would become the second American to win with an American horse, only months after Woodward's death.

Ironically (in light of the nature of his spat with Clark), Woodward would become a leading advocate for the repeal of the regulation passed in 1913 by the (English) Jockey Club (once called "the most exclusive gathering of men in the history of the free world, with the possible exception of the Last Supper") that refused to recognize most American pedigrees in the British *General Stud Book*.[17] The 1913 policy, colloquially known as the Jersey Act (in recognition of its author and chief proponent, Victor Child Villiers, Lord Jersey, chief steward of the English Jockey Club), had been passed in response to the glut of American Thoroughbreds flooding Great Britain in the early twentieth century, when state after state outlawed racing as part of a series of progressive reforms sweeping the United States. The British feared that the American horses would drive down prices for their own stock. Citing uncertainty about the genetic origins of many of the American horses, British racing leaders refused to recognize imported horses as "purebred" if their entire ancestry had not been so recognized. Though American horses were still allowed to race in Britain under the policy, the stigma associated with racing their "half-breeds" kept many top American owners away. In the aftermath of World War II and the decimation of European bloodstock that accompanied it, the British amended the Jersey Act to allow most American Thoroughbreds to be recognized in England.

The Jersey Act had not affected Clark's top filly, Galatea II, because she was descended entirely from "pure" European stock. After capturing the two English classics reserved for females (the One Thousand Guineas and the Oaks), Galatea II had been pointed toward the St. Leger Stakes, the oldest and longest of the English classics (and open to both colts and fillies) in 1939. But in light of the German invasion of Poland and Britain's subsequent declaration of war, the race was canceled for the only time in its history, which dated back to 1776. As the Germans stormed their way through Europe, Sterling evacuated his top equine stock. His Normandy estate would be used by the Germans as a cavalry station and would eventually be bombed by the Allies, but not before Sterling's top mare Galaday (dam of Galatea II and herself a top runner, in a career that included a third-place finish in the 1930 Kentucky Oaks) and her yearling daughter Boreale were evacuated aboard a ship that had delivered armaments to England.[18]

On American racetracks, Boreale never reached the potential that her mother's and sister's careers suggested, but she did win a New York race as a three-year-old before being retired. Man o' War's American Triple Crown–winning son War Admiral was chosen as a mate for Boreale because of his quality pedigree, a race record that placed him among the best American racehorses of the century, and his smallish size, which matched that of the mare. The result of that mating was Singing Grass, the mother of Never Say Die. Although Singing Grass remained a notch below the upper echelons of British racing, she would race successfully in England—seven wins in eighteen career starts—and demonstrated an ability to win at a distance, a trait she would pass on to her offspring.[19] Clark's equine manager in England, Gerald McElligott of the British Bloodstock Agency, recommended that Singing Grass be bred to Nasrullah, then standing in Ireland. Nasrullah represented the culmination of years of effort by his breeder—the immensely wealthy and powerful Aga Khan—to create the world's top racehorses and bloodlines.

In a relatively short time as an active participant in European racing, the Aga Khan had built the most successful racing and breeding stable in all of Europe. But none of his beloved animals would have a greater influence on Thoroughbred racing than his talented and temperamental runner Nasrullah. As a result of the mating of Nasrullah and Singing Grass, Robert Sterling Clark would reach the apex of the equine world in the autumn of his life with Never Say Die. But that moment would not have happened without the Aga Khan's passionate devotion to Thoroughbred racing and breeding. His fabulous wealth made it possible for him to become one of the most successful and influential breeders of Thoroughbreds in history. And the unusual origins of that wealth made him a relic of a vanishing aristocratic era in a quickly modernizing world.

Chapter 4

The Aga Khan

Sultan Mohammed Shah, the third Aga Khan, had been drawn to horses as long as he could remember. His earliest childhood memory was watching the horses of his grandfather, the first Aga Khan, participate in morning training while servants held him astride a pony in a saddle.[1] Eventually, the racehorses the Aga Khan bred and raced would leave a lasting impact on European record books and the Thoroughbred breed around the world.

As spiritual leaders of the roughly 15 million Nizari Ismaili Muslims—constituting the second-largest branch of Shia Islam—the Aga Khans trace their lineage directly back to the Prophet Mohammed through his daughter Fatima and her husband Ali. In addition to being the Prophet's son-in-law, Ali was his first cousin and close friend. As Mohammed was dying in the year 632, his followers assumed that Ali would succeed the Prophet as leader of the Muslim people. But when Mohammed became too sick to lead daily prayers and asked Abu-Bakr, the father of his favorite wife, to lead prayers in his stead, many interpreted this as a sign of the Prophet's intent that Abu-Bakr should succeed him. Upon Mohammed's death, two rival factions quickly formed. Modern-day Sunni Muslims are spiritual descendants of the followers of Abu-Bakr, who was chosen by a majority of followers from a group of elders to be the first Caliph ("successor"). The term *Sunni* derives from the Arabic word for "custom" or "usual habit." Supporters of Ali formed Shi'atu-Ali, Ali's party, or Shia for short.[2]

The split between Ismaili Shia and the great majority of Shia (called "Twelvers") occurred a century later in 732. Ismaili Muslims believe that Imam Jafar al-Sadiq, fearing for his eldest son Ismail's life, smuggled him to safety and staged a mock funeral for the boy. Twelver Muslims, claiming that Ismail was dead, pledged allegiance to Ismail's younger brother, Musa al-Kazim. Musa al-Kazim's line of succession continued until the twelfth imam, Mohammed al-Mahdi, who concealed himself upon ascending to power as a five-year-old in 874. The Twelvers are still waiting for him to reappear. The spiritual ancestors of modern Ismailis, who remained loyal to Ismail, were persecuted and forced to practice in secret, sending out clerics and missionaries from Syria and providing a model for later secret societies like the Freemasons.[3]

In the early tenth century, Imam Ubayd Allah al-Mahdi Billah claimed that he carried on the lineage of Ismail and that his predecessors had been operating in seclusion. Ubayd Allah established the Fatimid Empire, which would eventually encompass all of North Africa, much of the Middle East, and even parts of present-day Italy. The Fatimids founded the city of Cairo, from which they ruled a vast empire for two centuries, leaving a legacy of culture and learning that included Al-Azhar University. With the decline of the Fatimid Empire, the Ismailis established a Persian stronghold, which was toppled by Mongol invasion in the thirteenth century, forcing the Ismailis underground once again.

In 1817 the forty-fifth imam of the Ismailis was murdered in Persia under shady circumstances. In a gesture of goodwill and to distance himself from the incident, the Persian shah granted the son and successor of the murdered imam the honorary title of Aga Khan (Lord Chief) and offered the hand of his daughter in marriage. But relations between the Aga Khan and the

Persian leadership soon soured after a regime change, and the
Aga Khan was forced to flee following armed conflict. The Aga
Khan and a large cavalry force headed to Afghanistan, where the
British military was fighting the First Anglo-Afghan War. After
aiding the British in Kandahar, the Aga Khan led an attack on
Sindh in modern-day Pakistan. Unable to return to Persia, the
Aga Khan eventually settled in Bombay and was granted the title
His Highness by the British government. His family, accompa-
nied by an entourage of more than a thousand, eventually joined
him in India.

In Bombay the Aga Khan constructed the Aga Hall to serve
as the official center of the Imamate. He also built other seasonal
residences outside the city center. At the Aga Hall the Aga Khan
would receive thousands of pilgrims annually and collect tithes
and fees, including honoraria paid at weddings, funerals, and
other significant events, from all over the Muslim world. He also
provided food and shelter for many of his followers and associates on his palatial estates. He maintained a stable of racehorses,
many of which were top performers on the Bombay racecourse.
After ruling for sixty-four years, Aga Khan I died in 1881. His
son and successor, Aga Khan II, would rule for only four years
before dying from a chill caught on a hunting excursion.

Born at Honeymoon Lodge in Karachi in 1877, Aga Khan
III became the forty-eighth Ismaili imam at age seven, upon the
death of his father; he inherited the allegiance of millions of followers for whom he was expected to serve as spiritual leader and
secular adviser. A sickly, nearsighted, pudgy child, he received
a Jesuit education from European tutors that included an hour
of riding lessons after breakfast each morning. His childhood
was lavish and isolated inside the palace walls, which were sur-
rounded by ghastly poverty. His mother handled his financial inheritance adeptly, investing in mining interests, securities, and
land—including at least nine palaces on various royal estates
around India. She culled the stable of horses her son inherited

from his father and grandfather but kept enough top stock to ensure that the green and red racing silks of the Aga Khan were regularly spotted in the winner's circles of India's top race meets, including four straight victories in the Nizam Gold Cup, western India's most prestigious race.

As the Aga Khan was coming of age in the 1890s, the amicable paternalism that defined Indian-British relations during his childhood was giving way to condescending notions of the "white man's burden" and social Darwinism. Whereas upper-class Indians and Britons had warmly interacted at parties, on fields of play, and at racecourses in the 1880s, racial division and segregation were becoming increasingly rigid as the century came to a close. This shift coincided with the rise of the Indian National Congress, which demanded more autonomy for a growing Indian professional class and gave rise to increasing political unrest. The Aga Khan found himself receiving fewer social invitations from white elites, which exacerbated his already isolated existence.[4]

In November 1896 the Aga Khan married his first cousin in a sixteen-day wedding celebration that gave thousands of invited guests a diversion from the famine, plague, and Muslim-Hindi clashes that had engulfed large parts of India. It also provided thousands of laborers much-needed work in trying times. A 300-room palace was built to house special wedding guests, and dozens of giant tents were erected to shelter the overflow crowds that included Ismaili followers, Indian princes, and British dignitaries. Despite the pomp and circumstance that accompanied his wedding, the Aga Khan's marriage to his first begum was doomed from the beginning. He later blamed innocence and ignorance for their early sexual incompatibility, which became manifest on the wedding night and quickly led to estrangement.[5]

The Aga Khan had many servants but few friends in the palace. Rather than seeking solace among his followers, he increasingly turned his attention to what he perceived to be the world's center of culture and refinement—Europe. Within weeks it was clear that his marriage was a sham; within four months he was aboard a French ocean liner bound for Marseilles, attended by two servants. From Marseilles the twenty-year-old imam traveled to Nice, where Britain's Queen Victoria, monarch of the United Kingdom and Ireland and empress of India, was spending the season. He managed to obtain rooms near hers in the Hotel Excelsior Regina, and after repeated efforts to make himself conspicuous—and a note requesting an audience—the Aga Khan finally received an invitation to dine in Victoria's suite. Though he exchanged only a few words with her and was seated at the far end of the table, the Aga Khan was thrilled to be in the presence of British royalty and enjoyed the dinner thoroughly. Upon the queen's departure from Nice, the imam decided to move on to Paris. He loved the shop windows and jewelry stores of Nice and the casino and motorcar show in Monte Carlo, and he wanted to continue his exposure to the culture of Europe.[6]

In Paris the Aga Khan discovered the pleasures of European theater, women, museums, and horse racing. Some of his followers living in the area came to pay homage, but the hotel staff complained about the prostrated crowds that gathered in the hallways in the imam's absence. Soon he received a letter from England inviting him to visit Queen Victoria at Windsor Castle. After buying a solid gold elephant to present to Her Majesty, the Aga Khan departed for London, ready to immerse himself in the height of the city's social season. At the apex of the British imperial age, London was a center of power, prestige, culture, and leisure and the heart of the financial universe. Armed with his royal invitation, the Aga Khan was accepted into the social circles of the British aristocracy and the nouveaux riches, attending balls, garden parties, weekend retreats, and days at the races.

On the day he was to be received by the queen, the Aga Khan traveled to Windsor by train and was met by a carriage at the station. At the castle, Victoria received him in the audience room, where he was knighted without being required to kneel—a nod to his claim to regal lineage. Later, at a grand twelve-course dinner, Queen Victoria engaged the Aga Khan in conversation about India. Though he found the castle itself cold, he relished his experience as a guest of the queen.[7]

The Aga Khan was chosen by West Indian Muslims to represent them at the queen's Diamond Jubilee celebration in June, commemorating Victoria's sixty-year reign. Dressed in fine European clothes, he gave a speech on their behalf in which he pledged allegiance to the Crown and reminded his audience of the brave and loyal military service his grandfather had provided to Britain in Afghanistan and Sindh. In the procession through the streets of London, he rode in an open carriage among royalty from across Europe.

Still abuzz from these high times, the Aga Khan was in for a rude awakening when he got back to India. The bubonic plague had returned, killing thousands in and around Bombay. Though the outbreak had been contained, there was a pall over the city. The Aga Khan wore his traditional garb as he disembarked, but his traveling trunks were filled with Western fashions, and he soon hired a young Englishman to give him dancing lessons. Absence had not made his heart grow fonder for his begum; he ordered that separate quarters be built on his estate at Bombay's Malabar Hill, so the two would scarcely need to see each other. While he was committed to his duties as imam, his personal life was unfulfilling and lonely in India; within a few months, he was again bound for England.

London society was happy to receive the exotic and wealthy twenty-one-year-old playboy, and the Prince of Wales (soon to be King Edward VII) made the Aga Khan a member of his exclusive Marlborough Club. In the late spring of 1898 the imam attended his first Derby Stakes at Epsom, beginning a lifelong fascination with the race and the special atmosphere surrounding it. At the Derby he took a liking to a long shot named Jeddah. The colt's mother was Pilgrimage, and Jeddah was named after the Arabian city on the Red Sea that serves as a gateway to Mecca. Bookmakers were offering odds as high as 100–1 on Jeddah, and although his bet paid only 66–1, the Aga Khan's first Derby experience was a memorable one. Jeddah came from the back of the eighteen-horse field to catch the pacesetters 200 yards from the finish line. He held on for a three-quarter-length win that left the crowd dumbfounded. "I shall never all my life forget the thrill of my first Derby," he would later recall. "I stood there, gripping the rails as the horses thundered round Tattenham Corner and began to climb the hill."[8] His later experiences at the Derby would include five wins as an owner, a record that has never been bettered.

Aware of his success as an owner and breeder of Indian racehorses, the British royal family made note of the Aga Khan's growing interest in European racing and gave him access to the top racing circles in Britain. Queen Victoria presented the Aga Khan with a Royal Household badge for the exclusive Royal Enclosure at Ascot, a courtesy that would be extended to him throughout his life. The Prince of Wales arranged a tour of his stables at Sandringham for the imam, and the prince's racing adviser helped the Aga Khan register his racing colors with British racing authorities. Because the family's traditional green and red silks were already taken, he was given a chocolate and red pattern (though his successor would later manage to register green and red silks and carry on the Imamate's legacy on the British turf). Before being called back to India by his mother, the Aga Khan met with Germany's Kaiser Wilhelm II (Queen Victoria's grandson) at his palace in Potsdam to negotiate rice-growing concessions for his Ismaili people in East Africa. The Aga Khan left the meeting favorably impressed by Wilhelm and successful in his negotiations.

For the next couple of years the Aga Khan focused his attention on his people, as the start of the bloody Boer War in southern Africa put a damper on English society. In 1901, the year of King Edward VII's ascension to the throne, the Aga Khan was appointed to the Legislative Council of India, the ruling vice-roy's advisory board. The imam was a useful ally of the British: He was westward looking, rich, and influential in places where the British did not always have a secure hold on power. He was relatively well liked by both Hindu and Muslim Indians and was trusted by the British. Despite his obligations to his followers and his new foray into Indian politics, the Aga Khan managed to make the French Riviera his home away from home. He liked to gamble at Monte Carlo, entertain low-profile women, and attend Europe's best horse racing meets, but his position of leadership in India and around the Ismaili world kept him from completely immersing himself in the European lifestyle. For the time being, his entry into European horse racing as an owner and a breeder would have to wait.[9]

At the dawn of the twentieth century, Monte Carlo was a magnet for American heiresses looking for titles and titled Europeans looking for heiresses. It was a beacon of culture that attracted fans of opera, theater, and ballet, as well as casino gamblers and other hangers-on. There, while watching her perform in *Giselle*, the Aga fell in love with a nineteen-year-old Italian ballerina named Theresa "Ginetta" Magliano. He returned to the ballet the following night and later asked a friend in the press to arrange a meeting. Within weeks she was pregnant. The Aga Khan declared himself divorced from his first wife, but because his divorce would not be recognized in Europe, he arranged for a *muta* wedding in Egypt. Recognized under Shia Islam, *muta* marriages are contractual unions of a fixed term, the origins of which date back to the days when warriors might be separated from their "real" wives for long periods, creating the need for temporary or provisional ones. After her first pregnancy ended in miscarriage, Ginetta gave birth to a son, Mohammed Mahdi "Giuseppe" Khan, in Monte Carlo in 1909.[10]

At the funeral of King Edward VII the following year, the Aga Khan joined heads of state from around the world to honor the king. Days later, the Aga Khan received a telegram informing him that doctors feared his son was dying of spinal meningitis. He rushed back to Monte Carlo but arrived too late; his son did not live to see his second birthday. Ginetta was soon pregnant again with the child that would be named Aly Khan, and the Aga Khan returned to England to witness the coronation of King George V.

Though the new king did not share his father's enthusiasm for horse racing, George V and the Aga Khan shared a mutual interest in India.[11] Because of his increased power and popularity among Indian Muslims, the imam's significance to the British monarchy was growing. The Aga Khan's allegiance lay squarely with the Crown. He had been captivated by the royal family since his first encounter with Queen Victoria, and he valued the royal friendships he had forged in the years since. But the reasons for his allegiance became more complex as the threat of large-scale war grew darker in the early 1910s: the Aga Khan was concerned about the fate of his followers and all Muslims in the British Empire should Britain be weakened by a protracted conflict.

With that fear in mind, the Aga Khan embarked on a journey through Southeast Asia to spread the word to his people that he wanted them to adopt the customs and languages of the lands of their residence as completely as possible in all facets of life but religion. The Aga Khan practiced what he preached: he wore the clothes and accoutrements of a European gentleman and spoke at least five European languages fluently. While at sea bound for Burma, he received the news that Archduke Franz Ferdinand had been assassinated in Sarajevo. After delivering his speech as scheduled in Burma, the Aga Khan traveled to Zanzibar, where he learned from the British resident governor that Britain had declared war on Germany. From Zanzibar the Aga Khan quickly headed to England via South Africa and met with Lord Kitchener, Britain's secretary of state for war, to pledge his allegiance and offer his services to the Crown. Lord Kitchener asked the

Aga Khan to use his influence and contacts to convince Muslims to resist the calls for jihad that were emanating from Turkey, which had entered into an Ottoman-German alliance and was encouraging all Muslims to oppose Britain and its allies.[12] While it is difficult to determine just how much influence the Aga Khan had, Muslims in the British Empire largely ignored the calls for jihad. As a result, the Aga Khan won acclaim from the British population for his efforts.

Because of his high profile, the Aga Khan feared reprisal from the Germans and moved his family to Switzerland. While there he was diagnosed with Graves' disease, which is marked by an overactive thyroid. His doctor told him to avoid caffeine, which allowed him to survive an assassination attempt when a German agent, dressed as a servant, placed poison in his coffee at a dinner party. This near miss came on the heels of another scare when a bomb thrown at his moving car had failed to explode. Finding that Switzerland was not as safe as he had imagined, the Aga Khan returned to France, where he remained for the duration of the war, which had already become the costliest and bloodiest in recorded history.

In 1919, with peace restored to Europe, the Aga Khan attended the English Derby at Epsom for the first time since the war began. For the next two years he did not miss a major race in Europe or India. Then, while attending a dinner in 1921, the Aga Khan found himself seated next to a serious racing enthusiast, a daughter-in-law of former British prime minister Herbert Asquith. The pair talked horse racing throughout their meal and continued the conversation afterward.[13] It was then that the Aga Khan realized he wanted to race Thoroughbreds in Europe at the highest levels. "It was like a trigger being drawn on a cannon," he recalled. "What was pent up from childhood and would never have come out suddenly became an irresistible mental storm."[14] At the conclusion of their conversation, the Aga Khan's dinner partner gave him contact information for her brother-in-law, legendary British trainer George Lambton. The imam wrote to Lambton the following day, and the trainer told the imam that although he was not looking for new clients, he would help him buy a few horses.[15] The Aga Khan was on his way to creating one of the most successful and influential Thoroughbred racing and breeding stables in history.

Chapter 5

Robber Barons
Robbing Barons

In 1922 the Doncaster sales grounds in South Yorkshire, England, were abuzz with talk of an impeccably bred filly whose looks matched her regal pedigree. Agents of all the top owners were in attendance, including trainer George Lambton, who had agreed to purchase a few young racehorses for the Aga Khan to help him fill his nascent racing stable. The filly that was catching everyone's eye shared the coloring of her sire, The Tetrarch, whose gray coat had looked like it had been speckled with whitewash. Though his unusual color and gangly appearance had garnered snickers in the saddling paddock before his first race at Newmarket some nine years earlier (at a time when gray horses were considered inferior genetic oddities), The Tetrarch turned doubters into believers when he won his debut by four easy lengths, routing the field of twenty-one starters. Those who had compared him to a rocking horse prior to his debut were soon calling him the "Spotted Wonder."[1] In his next start, The Tetrarch put away his rivals after a quarter mile in the six-furlong Woodcote Stakes at Epsom. He followed that performance with a stakes win at Royal Ascot in which his nearest competitor finished ten lengths behind. The Tetrarch continued his winning ways with stakes wins at Sandown, Derby, Goodwood, and Doncaster that summer.

In October, as The Tetrarch was coming to the end of one of the most remarkable two-year-old seasons in the history of racing, he injured himself during morning training when his right hind foot grabbed his right front ankle. The horse had a tremendous "overstride," which allowed him to reach great speed when running at a full gallop. But when he slowed up, he had the propensity to nick the back of his front legs with his hind feet, which is what happened in this case. Despite the injury, he was heavily favored in early betting on the Epsom Derby to be run the following spring. Though he had never carried his speed beyond sprint distances, The Tetrarch was so dominant at shorter distances that punters believed his form would transfer to longer races as well. Unfortunately, while training for his spring debut, the colt suffered another similar injury, this time rupturing a tendon and ending his career. He retired with an unblemished seven-for-seven record.

His jockey for all seven races was Steve Donoghue, who explained that The Tetrarch "combined the power of an elephant with the speed of a greyhound."[2] The colt was retired to the breeding shed, where he sired only 130 foals because of a serious lack of libido. His owner called his attitude toward sex "monastic in the extreme."[3] Though limited in number, his offspring did have success on the racetrack; he sired 80 winners from those 130 foals and was even champion sire of 1919. The fact that three of his winners won Britain's longest classic race, the St. Leger, suggests that The Tetrarch may well have thrived at longer distances. But none of his other offspring was as brilliant as the gray filly out of Lady Josephine that was the talk of the 1922 Doncaster yearling sales.

The 9,100 guineas George Lambton paid for the spotted gray filly on behalf of the Aga Khan was a near-record price. But she proved to be worth every shilling. The Aga Khan named her

Mumtaz Mahal ("chosen one of the palace") after the favorite wife of Emperor Shah Jahan, who built the Taj Mahal in the seventeenth century in her memory after her untimely death during childbirth. Upon making the purchase, Lambton said of Mumtaz Mahal, "As an individual she is wonderful, as near perfection as imagination can conceive. Her conformation is ideal and she has both size and quality." But, in an attempt to dampen any unreasonable expectations, he added, "This does not necessarily mean she is bound to be a racing paragon."[4]

In fact, she *was* a racing paragon. She was sent to trainer Dick Dawson's Whatcome Stable in Oxfordshire, and Dawson thought highly enough of Mumtaz Mahal to enter her in the Spring Stakes at Newmarket for her career debut as a two-year-old. The filly justified her trainer's faith by setting a new course record: 57 4/5 seconds for five furlongs. Next time out she won the Queen Mary Stakes at Ascot by ten lengths, earning the nickname the "Flying Filly," which she would retain for the rest of her life. She was never seriously challenged in her next three wins and suffered her only defeat of the year in her final start as a two-year-old in the Imperial Produce Stakes at Kempton. A prerace downpour had left the course heavy, which was not to the Flying Filly's liking. Though she lost to a colt named Arcade that day, she was still named top two-year-old of the year and, like her sire The Tetrarch, was being called one of the fastest horses anyone had ever seen. For winter rest she was sent to Lord Carnarvon's Highclere Stud, which was owned by the son of the recently deceased 5th Earl of Carnarvon, who had died under mysterious circumstances after funding the excavation of King Tutankhamen's tomb in Egypt.

The following spring, Mumtaz Mahal returned for the year's first British classic for fillies, the One Thousand Guineas, contested at a mile on the straight course at Newmarket in early May. There were some legitimate concerns going into the race about the Flying Filly's capability of carrying her speed as far as a mile. Though some of his progeny had success at longer distances, The Tetrarch had never run past six furlongs, and Mumtaz Mahal's dam, Lady Josephine, was a precocious sprinter who had never shown a propensity to stretch past sprinting distances.

Mumtaz Mahal ran well enough to finish second in the Guineas, but it took a fifth-place finish in her next start in the one-mile Coronation Stakes at Ascot to convince her owner and trainer that she should be left to sprinting. She finished her racing career with a pair of wins in two sprint stakes at Goodwood and York, retiring to the Aga Khan's farm at the Curragh (an ancient open plain in County Kildare, Ireland) with an impressive seven wins and two seconds in her ten career starts. More than her race record, racing fans who saw Mumtaz Mahal at her best would remember her as one of the fastest and most visually impressive horses in the sport's history. Largely on the strength of the Flying Filly's remarkable year, the Aga Khan won the first of his thirteen titles as leading owner in Great Britain in 1924.[5] Though pleased with his early success, the Aga Khan made winning the English Derby at Epsom the top priority for his stable.

In 1926 the Aga Khan's wife, Ginetta, died in Paris from complications of surgery. Three years later he married his longtime mistress, French clothing designer Andrée Caron. The following June, the Aga Khan had two starters in the Epsom Derby. On Derby Day he was accompanied to the races by his son, Aly, because his new wife had not yet been recognized by the Court (due in part to lingering rumors regarding the legality of their marriage) and thus could not enter the Royal Enclosure. Of his two starters, Rustom Pasha was considered the most likely candidate for a Derby triumph. The second horse, Blenheim, had shown serious promise the previous year as a two-year-old, earning four wins and two second-place finishes in his seven starts, but he had not managed to reproduce that form in the first two starts of his three-year-old season. The stable's top jockey chose to ride Rustom Pasha rather than Blenheim in the Derby, and bettors seemed to agree with his decision, making Rustom Pasha the second favorite at odds of 9–2, while ignoring Blenheim at 18–1.

Although Rustom Pasha faded early, Blenheim emerged from the back of the pack in the late going under the urging of jockey Harry Wragg to win by a length. When the notoriously nearsighted Aga Khan saw his colors streaking toward the finish line in front, even he thought it was Rustom Pasha. Though Blenheim would be injured while training for his next race, forcing his retirement, he would go on to have a long and successful stud career.

Blenheim was sent to France for stud duty, where he got off to a tremendous start. His son Mahmoud (owned and bred by the Aga Khan) broke the stakes record in the Derby in 1936, making Blenheim a seriously hot commodity. When news broke that the Aga Khan had agreed to sell the stallion at the height of his popularity in 1936 to an American syndicate for a reported quarter-million dollars, he was widely criticized by British race fans and horsemen.[6] Lord Derby even went so far as to refuse to breed his stallions to the Aga Khan's mares because of his disappointment in the imam's decision to export his top sire.

The Aga Khan responded to the criticism in the *Daily Telegraph*, defending himself by claiming that "no one is a greater or more loyal supporter of British bloodstock and racing, and all that it means."[7] The Aga Khan was certainly a great supporter of British racing, but in exporting his promising young sire, he was exposing his horse to a growing American market, where racing was expanding. And although he was one of the world's wealthiest men, he was also a businessman (and a man burdened with both expensive tastes and the responsibility of helping to provide for millions of his followers). He was a sportsman who was committed to racing and breeding top horses, but he also tried to offset his tremendous equine-related expenses with income whenever a good opportunity presented itself.

The sale of Blenheim to American interests struck at British breeders' pride, but by the 1930s, American stud farms were emerging, with financial backing from top American breeders with vast fortunes based in American industry and finance, to challenge the British and French positions in the international pecking order for top stallion prospects. Whether or not the British racing aristocracy cared to admit it, the Thoroughbred world was changing. One important development was that American racing was indirectly benefiting from the economic woes of the Great Depression, as state after state legalized pari-mutuel wagering—and, by implication, Thoroughbred racing—as a way to increase foundering tax revenues. Top American breeders recognized that the stallion business had real profit potential and were willing to expend serious amounts of money to secure Europe's best horses for the American breeding market.

The American syndicate that bought Blenheim included some of the most wealthy and influential Thoroughbred breeders of the day. It was organized by Kentucky horseman Arthur B. Hancock, called upon his death "probably the most influential breeder in the history of the American Turf" by the *Bloodstock Breeders' Review*.[8] Hancock began his equine career on Ellerslie Farm outside Charlottesville, Virginia, helping his father raise racehorses on land belonging to his mother's family. Hancock expanded his operation when his own wife inherited 1,300 acres of central Kentucky farmland in 1910, which became Claiborne Farm. By the 1920s, he was boarding horses for and advising some of the most successful American sportsmen of the day.

To purchase Blenheim (who would be known as Blenheim II in America because of the existence of another horse by the same name), Hancock gathered some of his contacts to form a syndicate. They included Warren Wright Sr., heir to his father's baking powder fortune and owner of Calumet Farm in Lexington, Kentucky, which would establish an unmatched record of dominance in American racing and breeding in the 1940s and

Some of the top European stallion prospects were imported to America to stand at Claiborne Farm, including Sir Gallahad III, Blenheim II, and Nasrullah, sire of Never Say Die. (Courtesy of University of Kentucky Archives)

1950s; Slovakian immigrant John D. Hertz, who created a taxi-cab and rental car empire and owned 1928 Kentucky Derby winner Reigh Count, who would sire Hertz's 1943 American Triple Crown winner Count Fleet, one of the greatest American runners of the twentieth century; and members of the wealthy Du Pont and Whitney families. These prominent breeders exemplified a wealthy class of Americans that, beginning in the late nineteenth century, had participated in American racing at the highest levels and helped drive the visibility and popularity of horse racing in American culture. Blenheim was immediately successful upon moving to America, siring American Triple Crown champion Whirlaway for Calumet Farm in his very first crop.

In exporting his top sire to America, the Aga Khan was part of an emerging trend. Americans had imported British stallions for centuries, but they were usually second-rate horses, solid runners that had not panned out as stallions, or good stallions believed to be past their prime. The first imported European stal-

Whirlaway winning the 1941 American Triple Crown. One of the greatest American racehorses of the twentieth century, Whirlaway was part of Blenheim II's first American crop. (Keeneland Library)

lion to have a major influence on the Thoroughbred breed in America was the winner of the first Epsom Derby, Diomed. Diomed was among the greatest racehorses ever seen in Britain, but he failed to live up to his billing as a stallion for owner Charles Bunbury. By the age of twenty-one, Diomed was getting few takers at a stud fee of only two guineas. Despite the brilliant runner's dismal record at stud, a Virginia breeder named Colonel John Hoomes saw an opportunity and bought Diomed for $250 in 1798. Hoomes imported the stallion to America and later sold him for a tidy profit.[9] Diomed had a prolific career at stud in the United States, covering mares right up until his death ten years later. Through his son Sir Archy, Diomed's descendants would dominate the American turf for the next century.

The first great commercial stallion of the central Kentucky bluegrass region was Sir Archy's great-grandson Lexington, who was the leading American sire sixteen times from 1861 to 1878, standing at Robert A. Alexander's Woodburn Farm in Woodford County. The *Kentucky Live Stock Record* recalled (perhaps hy-

Lexington, the leading sire in North America sixteen times in the late nineteenth century, enhanced central Kentucky's reputation as an important commercial Thoroughbred breeding center. (Courtesy of University of Kentucky Archives)

perbolically) of Lexington, "As a race horse, he stands pre-eminently the best this country has ever produced, and as a stallion he takes rank as the foremost in the world. He was far superior to all the horses that have gone before him, as the brilliancy of the sun is superior to the glimmer of the most distant star."[10] Lexington (the horse) helped establish central Kentucky as a center of the American Thoroughbred industry, but his American pedigree caused his offspring to be considered "half-breeds" in Britain following passage of the 1913 Jersey Act.

William Collins Whitney, patriarch of the famous racing family, had success with another hard-luck stallion imported from England in 1893 named Meddler. Whitney was a prosperous lawyer before serving as secretary of the navy in President Grover Cleveland's first administration. As secretary, Whitney helped modernize the U.S. Navy by spearheading an effort to equip wooden warships with armor plating. He became very wealthy as a result of his involvement in the consolidation of the

New York City train system and the creation of the American Tobacco Company and his heavy investment in the energy company that would later be known as Consolidated Edison. Whitney also benefited (though not as directly as his children would, through inheritance) from his association with his wife's brother, Oliver Hazard Payne, one of the wealthiest men in America. Payne had made a fortune through his involvement with the American Tobacco Company, Standard Oil, and U.S. Steel, all amid rumors of political maneuvering that today might be called "chicanery" but at the time was merely part of "doing business" in the United States.

As a racehorse, Meddler was undefeated as a two-year-old in 1892. By a Derby winner, out of an Oaks winner, Meddler appeared to be destined for historical greatness. But his owner died, and according to rules in place at the time, Meddler was no longer eligible to compete in races to which the deceased owner had nominated him. A Massachusetts breeder named William H. Forbes (who had provided significant financial backing for Alexander Graham Bell's telephone and became president of American Bell Telephone Company) spotted an opportunity. Forbes, a son-in-law of American essayist Ralph Waldo Emerson and father of a future governor-general of the Philippines, bought Meddler at auction in Newmarket for 14,500 guineas and brought him to America in the summer of 1893. Upon Forbes's untimely death before the end of the century, Meddler was acquired by Whitney and sent to his stud farm near Lexington.[11] Meddler would twice be the leading sire in North America, in 1904 and 1906, bracketing an appearance atop the sire list by another Whitney-owned stallion—Hamburg.

The first influential stallion imported to America in the twentieth century was Star Shoot. As a young foal in Ireland, he had survived a nasty fever with the help of a groom, who wrapped the colt in blankets and warmed him by a tack-room fireplace. On the racetrack, Star Shoot won three stakes races as

Imported from Britain in 1901, Star Shoot was the leading North American sire five times from 1911 to 1919. Among his most notable offspring was the first American Triple Crown winner, Sir Barton. (Courtesy of University of Kentucky Archives)

a two-year-old but then developed a breathing problem and was retired. The British were extremely wary of breeding to a horse that had demonstrated wind problems, so he was shipped off to America. Standing first at Runnymede Farm in Paris, Kentucky, and later at John E. Madden's Hamburg Place in Lexington, Star Shoot became the first dominant sire of the twentieth century in America, leading the American sire list five times and siring sixty-one stakes winners, including the first American Triple Crown winner, Sir Barton. Today, Star Shoot and Sir Barton are memorialized with streets named in their honor that run through the land formerly occupied by Hamburg Place, where Never Say Die would be born and raised and where now sits an enormous shopping center and residential development that also bears the name Hamburg.

Impressed with the success of Star Shoot, and armed with capital from an economy spared the destruction World War I had wreaked in Europe, Arthur Hancock organized a small group

Imported from France in 1926, Sir Gallahad III sired American Triple Crown winner Gallant Fox in his first American crop. He would lead the North American broodmare sire list a record twelve times. (Courtesy of Claiborne Farm)

that included William Woodward and Marshall Field III (heir to the Chicago department store fortune) to purchase top French runner Sir Gallahad (he would be registered as Sir Gallahad III in the United States) for $125,000 in 1926. Woodward—the future Jockey Club chairman with whom Robert Sterling Clark would have a fateful clash—was part of a wealthy New York City family that had made its fortune selling textiles to the Confederate government. After graduating from Harvard Law School, Woodward served as secretary to the American ambassador to Great Britain, where he developed a lifelong love of English sport. Upon his return to the States, Woodward landed a job at Hanover National Bank in New York, where his uncle (a lifelong bachelor) was president. When his uncle died a few years later,

Woodward took over the bank presidency and inherited Belair Stud in Maryland.[12]

Sir Gallahad possessed a number of traits that Hancock, Woodward, and their partners thought would make him a top sire: he had shown precocity by winning multiple stakes at age two, class by winning the French Two Thousand Guineas, speed by beating top French sprinter Epinard in a stakes race, and even some stamina by finishing a close third in the French Derby. Americans had imported useful stallions from Europe in the past, but Sir Gallahad turned out to be a great stallion, justifying the syndicate's faith. He topped the North American general sire list four times from 1930 to 1940, sired three Kentucky Derby winners, and led the North American broodmare sire list a record twelve times. In Sir Gallahad's very first American crop, he sired a Triple Crown champion for William Woodward in Gallant Fox, one of the top American runners of the twentieth century. As mentioned, that feat would be matched by Blenheim, who sired Calumet's Triple Crown winner Whirlaway in his first American crop. The syndicate structure of stallion ownership gave breeders incentive to breed their top mares to stallions they co-owned, and with a large number of wealthy American businesspersons and their heirs participating in Thoroughbred racing and breeding in the first half of the twentieth century, the financial clout of American stallion syndicates was quite formidable.

As Gallant Fox was streaking to the American Triple Crown in 1930, demands for self-rule in India prompted the British government to hold the first of a series of Roundtable Conferences, chaired by Prime Minister Ramsay MacDonald, to discuss the possibility of dominion status for India and the protection of minorities' rights in a hypothetically autonomous India. The Aga Khan was chosen to represent the All-India Muslim League at the conference, but the talks bore little fruit because the powerful Indian National Congress refused to attend; its leaders were protesting Mohandas Gandhi's imprisonment for civil disobedience in India. The following year, after much negotiation, Gandhi appeared in London for a second conference. He demanded complete independence for India and equal status with Britain (demands that, in hindsight, were harbingers of the imminent disintegration of the British Empire in the coming decades). Talks at St. James's Palace quickly broke down, and the Aga Khan, who favored a more gradual move toward autonomy for India, invited Gandhi to his private suite at the Ritz Hotel for more intimate discussions. But the imam had no luck in finding any middle ground with Gandhi, and the second conference ended without any real breakthrough.[13]

Though he was heavily involved in matters of political and diplomatic significance, the Aga Khan's mind was never far from horse racing. Before sending Blenheim to America, the Aga Khan bred Mumtaz Mahal to his Derby champion, hoping that Blenheim's ability at the Derby distance of 1½ miles, combined with Mumtaz Mahal's legendary speed, would produce a special equine athlete. Though she failed to live up to the promise of her pedigree (on the racecourse, anyway), the resulting foal, named Mumtaz Begum, showed some precocity, winning twice in England as a two-year-old before being sent to the breeding shed at age three. After limited success with her early offspring, the Aga Khan decided to breed Mumtaz Begum to the undefeated Italian champion Nearco, a decision that would have lasting repercussions for the Thoroughbred breed.

Nearco was the product of a quarter century of horse breeding by Italian horseman Federico Tesio, arguably the most influential breeder of Thoroughbreds in the twentieth century. Born in Turin, Tesio had been orphaned at a young age and was educated at the nearby Barnabite College at Moncalieri. There, Father Francesco Denza, a renowned astronomer, instilled in Tesio a love of science and introduced him to the theories of Charles Darwin and pioneering geneticist Gregor Mendel. After inheriting a bit of money (and, according to popular legend, creating a scandal when he surprised a married woman he was trying to seduce by popping through her hotel window in Pisa), Tesio embarked on a journey around the world that included a stint as a gentleman jockey in Europe, a jaunt across the Argentine pampas with a herd of horses, and an expedition through Patagonia on horseback, before finally returning to Italy. There he fell in love with and married Donna Lydia Flori di Serramezzana, an expert horsewoman whose Dalmatian family had been prosperous in the shipping industry. The pair soon established Dormello Stud on Lake Maggiore, in the piedmont region of northern Italy. Eventually, Tesio would breed and raise nearly two dozen winners of the Italian Derby (many of which he also owned and trained). But in the absence of the financial means to compete with the nobility of Italian racing, Tesio's progress toward the top of the sport was slow.

By the early 1910s, Tesio had already enjoyed some success on the Italian turf, including a victory in the 1912 Italian Derby, but his legacy as one of the greatest breeders in the history of horse racing would begin with his 1915 purchase of a "mournful, light-boned filly" named Catnip, whom he purchased at auction in England.[14] Though she had won only once in her ten career starts, both her sire and dam were English classic winners, and Tesio thought Catnip was a steal at only seventy-five guineas. English locals thought Tesio was "not only foreign, but possibly mad" for taking a chance on the filly, but he soon proved them wrong.[15]

Catnip's daughter Nogara won two Italian classics for Tesio, and following her retirement, the horseman carefully deliberated about which stallion would make the perfect match for the small, compact filly. He decided on Fairway, a tall, lanky stallion that had won the St. Leger Stakes for his owner, Lord Derby. But by the time he made the decision, Fairway's book was full for that year, and Tesio had to settle for his full brother, Pharos, a decidedly smaller horse that was in far less demand as a stallion. The result of the mating was a stocky, dark bay colt named Nearco.

A bully in his paddock as a youngster, Nearco was all business on the racecourse. He won his first race at Italy's San Siro racecourse in June and then won six races in as many attempts in the fall. The next year, Nearco captured victory in his first six races as a three-year-old, including the Italian Two Thousand Guineas and the Italian Derby, running his career record to a perfect thirteen for thirteen. Even though he had won every race he entered, at distances from five furlongs to 1½ miles, detractors could correctly claim that Nearco had never raced outside Italy. To improve his value as a stallion, Tesio would have to show that Nearco could compete with the best horses in Europe, and he eyed the Grand Prix de Paris at Longchamp as an opportunity to prove that Nearco was indeed the greatest horse of his generation. Tesio sought and received permission from fascist dictator Benito Mussolini to take his horse out of the country for the big race.

At Longchamp, Nearco faced the greatest three-year-olds of Europe, including the winners of the French and English Derbies, as well as the top European three-year-old filly of the year. Nearco's jockey, Gubblini, kept the horse forwardly placed and out of trouble in the early going of the long 1⅞-mile race.[16] When Gubblini urged Nearco with six furlongs to go, the colt responded and won by a comfortable length.

On the way back to the paddock, Nearco was excitedly cheered by a vocal group of Italians amid the large French crowd, which was not happy with the results of the race. When the jockey issued a fascist salute to the French, it set off a firestorm of jeers, but the horse and his handlers managed to escape the scene physically unharmed. Nearco never made it back to Italy, however. Days after his historic triumph, Tesio sold him (against Mussolini's orders) to Martin H. Benson, a British bookmaker, for a record 60,000 pounds. With a perfect record of fourteen wins in fourteen starts, Nearco was retired to Benson's Beech House Stud near Newmarket, where an underground bomb shelter would be installed in the paddock to protect Nearco from the German aerial assault on Britain, and where the Aga Khan would send his mare Mumtaz Begum to be bred to the great champion the following year.

As the testy postrace exchange between French race fans and the Italian jockey illustrated, Europe again stood on the brink of war. The Aga Khan continued to represent his Ismaili people and the British Empire in the increasingly tense diplomatic realm. In 1937 and 1938 he served as president of the League of Nations, whose attention was focused squarely on the looming threat of Adolf Hitler and the Nazi Party in Germany. The Aga Khan had been favorably impressed with the Führer in his brief meetings with Hitler, and he voiced support for German *Anschluss* with Austria, suggesting that the dictator should be taken at his word regarding his lack of imperial ambitions.[17] His faith soon proved to be much misplaced.

The Nazi march across Europe disrupted all facets of life on the Continent, and the sport of horse racing was certainly no exception. The Germans seized thousands of horses, including many of the Aga Khan's French stock. Despite the disruptions, the sport of racing and the business of breeding persevered, albeit in a very limited fashion. The Aga Khan kept track of his beloved racehorses as best he could while taking refuge in the Palace Hotel in Saint Moritz, Switzerland. Unable to access most of his immense global assets (which by this time included African mining interests, Asian manufacturing enterprises, a publishing conglomerate, various equine operations in France and Ireland, oil and real estate holdings, numerous residences, and priceless antiques and pieces of art), he was forced to sell his Derby-winning stallions Mahmoud and Bahram to American interests to raise some liquid capital to finance his lavish lifestyle. Cash could be hard to come by amid wartime restrictions, even for someone as powerful and influential as the Aga Khan.

Winner of the 1936 Epsom Derby for his owner Aga Khan III, Mahmoud was sold to Cornelius Vanderbilt Whitney in 1940 and stood at Whitney's stud farm outside Lexington, Kentucky, where he became a champion sire and champion broodmare sire. (Courtesy of University of Kentucky Archives)

Cornelius Vanderbilt Whitney, a grandson of William Collins Whitney, purchased Mahmoud for a reported $84,000.[18] The son of American sportsman Harry Payne Whitney and artist and patron of the arts Gertrude Vanderbilt, C. V. Whitney inherited vast sums of money from both sides of his family. He made a name for himself in his own right as a founder of Pan American Airlines and as a financier of Hollywood films, including *Gone with the Wind* and *The Searchers*. Whitney stood Mahmoud, the son of Blenheim and grandson of the Flying Filly, at his farm near Lexington, where the stallion would enjoy solid success, including a spot at the top of the North American sire list in 1946. Mahmoud's influence on the Thoroughbred breed lives on through the ubiquitous Halo and Northern Dancer stallion lines

A misbehaving underachiever on the racecourse for his owner, Aga Khan III, Nasrullah became one of the most influential sires of the twentieth century and was the first stallion to top both the British and North American sire lists. (Painting by Milton Menasco, courtesy of Claiborne Farm)

today, but he was fortunate to make it to the United States at all. As he was being loaded on a ship for his transatlantic voyage, the captain refused to allow the horse to board for want of proper documentation. That ship was torpedoed in the Atlantic. Mahmoud was forced to wait for the next ship, which made its crossing safely and without incident.

As war raged in Europe early in 1940, the Aga Khan's mare Mumtaz Begum, daughter of the Flying Filly, gave birth to her Nearco foal at the imam's farm in County Kildare, Ireland. Named Nasrullah (Arabic for "victory of God"), the colt would eventually become one of the most influential stallions in history, siring ninety-eight stakes winners—including Never Say Die— and would permanently alter the global Thoroughbred breeding industry. But the only thing that was clear from his early performances on the racetrack was that he had both tremendous talent and a quirky temperament, which would keep him from living up to his immense potential as a racehorse.

After a promising two-year-old season that included a victory in the Coventry Stakes, Nasrullah began his three-year-old campaign in the Chatteris Stakes, which he won despite easing up noticeably once he took the lead. His next race was the Two Thousand Guineas at Newmarket, where, prior to the race, Nasrullah caused another round of frustration when he simply refused to budge upon leaving the saddling enclosure. Eventually, he was convinced to make his way toward the starting line, but he demonstrated his pigheadedness during the race itself when, upon gaining the lead not far from the finish line, Nasrullah slowed down demonstrably, even though trainer Frank Butters had added blinkers (unusual in England at the time), which were supposed to help keep the horse focused on the task at hand. After a third-place finish at the Derby Stakes (run at Newmarket during the war because Epsom was needed for military purposes), some critics questioned his stamina. But with his win in the 1¼-mile Champion Stakes over older horses later that fall, those questions were answered.

Jockey Sir Gordon Richards finally identified the best strategy for managing Nasrullah on the racetrack: timing his late run to end precisely at the finish line. Richards later admitted that the colt was a challenge, recalling that Nasrullah "was very, very difficult to ride."[19] The jockey theorized that part of the colt's problem was boredom, as he was forced to run over the same racetrack due to wartime restrictions. But given his propensity for bullheadedness in other environments, it is safe to say that the colt would have been a handful on any racecourse.

Throughout his career, Nasrullah gave his handlers and supporters fits. The *Raceform* notes describing his racetrack performances are reminiscent of a delinquent child's report card and illustrate Nasrullah's penchant for misbehavior: "no resolution under pressure," "veered right," "willful in paddock," "darted left," and "not keen under pressure" are some examples.[20] Racing commentator Phil Bull begrudgingly gave the disappointing Nasrullah a place in his *Best Horses of 1943* publication, explaining that "in spite of his having failed in each of his classic ventures, in spite of his bad temper, his mulish antics, in spite of his exasperating unwillingness to do the job, etc., etc., I fear that I am going to give him another write up. I know he doesn't deserve it, but I can't help it." Bull continued, "Personally, I have to announce that I still persist, with a pig-headed obstinacy equal only to that of Nasrullah himself, in the firm opinion that (up to 1½ miles) the son of Nearco was head and shoulders above his contemporaries *in ability*." Bull concluded his analysis of Nasrullah with a prescient observation about the colt's future prospects: "If conformation and innate ability count for anything he may make [a] name for himself as a stallion which his unfortunate temperament prevented his making for himself as a racehorse."[21]

Upon Nasrullah's retirement, despite his fine pedigree and his propensity for brilliance on the racetrack, some breeders were reticent to breed to him, given his temperament. Irishman Joseph McGrath, who had turned his focus to racehorses after a political career that included membership in the Irish Republican Army and Sinn Fein and participation in the 1916 Easter Rising, was willing to take a chance on Nasrullah and purchased the stallion. With Continental Europe still languishing in total war, the Aga Khan was a willing seller. Nasrullah stood at Barton Stud in Suffolk, England, for a year before moving to McGrath's Brownstown Stud in County Kildare, Ireland.[22]

The fateful mating of Nasrullah with Robert Sterling Clark's Singing Grass, which would produce Never Say Die, took place at Brownstown in what would be Nasrullah's final season in Ireland. At the conclusion of the breeding season, Nasrullah was purchased for $340,000 by a syndicate of top American breed-

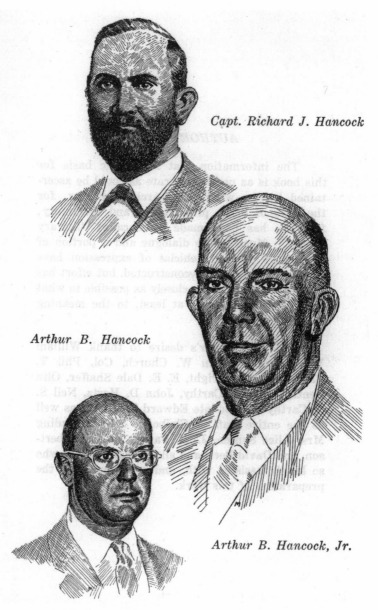

Capt. Richard J. Hancock

Arthur B. Hancock

Arthur B. Hancock, Jr.

Three generations of Hancocks. Captain Richard Hancock raised Thoroughbreds in Virginia after serving in the Confederate Army. His son, Arthur B. Hancock, established Claiborne Farm near Paris, Kentucky, and Arthur B. "Bull" Hancock Jr. carried on his father's legacy of importing and standing some of the top stallions in America. (Courtesy of Claiborne Farm)

ers organized by Arthur Hancock's son, Arthur "Bull" Hancock Jr., and was moved to Kentucky to stand at Claiborne Farm, where he would have access to some of the best broodmares in America.[23] The syndicate included some of the biggest names in American racing: William Woodward; John D. Hertz; publisher, diplomat, and businessman Harry F. Guggenheim; financier Henry Carnegie Phipps; Clifford Mooers, proprietor of Walnut Springs, the central Kentucky farm briefly owned by Sterling Clark; and George D. Widener Jr., who grew up in "Lynnewood Hall," the 110-room mansion built by his streetcar-magnate grandfather outside Philadelphia.

As a sire, Nasrullah had already shown plenty of promise in England and was arguably the highest-profile stallion ever imported to the United States. In 1950, the year Nasrullah arrived in America, his son Noor had historic success in California after beginning his career on the English turf. Bred in Ireland by the Aga Khan, Noor (Arabic for "light") became the first horse to defeat two American Triple Crown winners in the same year. He beat Citation four straight times earlier in the year before trouncing 1946 American Triple Crown winner Assault twice in eight days to cap off a remarkable season.[24] The following year, Nasrullah's runners in England were even better, garnering him champion sire honors and raising American expectations even further. In his first American crop, Nasrullah sired future Hall of Famer Nashua, a champion at two and three. Nashua retired as the all-time leading earner in the history of American racing and would later be syndicated for over $1.2 million in a then-record deal—a mere hint of the astronomical heights the American bloodstock market would later reach.

Though he failed to live up to his tremendous potential on the racetrack, Nasrullah would eventually become his breeder's greatest equine legacy, earning immortality as part of the story of the Aga Khan's remarkable life of accomplishment, influence, acquisition, and experience. Nasrullah would become the first

Nasrullah's son Noor finished third in the 1948 Epsom Derby but found greater success in America after being sold to Charles Howard, owner of Seabiscuit. In 1950 Noor earned champion older male honors after defeating two American Triple Crown winners, Citation and Assault, on multiple occasions. (Keeneland Library)

stallion to top both the American and the British sire lists, siring an astounding 23 percent stakes winners from his foals, including nine American champions.[25] His male-line descendants, including Nashua, Bold Ruler, Secretariat, Seattle Slew, and A. P. Indy, would leave indelible marks on the racetrack record books and on the Thoroughbred breed itself. But all those accomplishments and accolades would come after Never Say Die's Derby triumph, giving credence to Federico Tesio's famous declaration: "The Thoroughbred racehorse exists because its selection has depended not on experts, technicians or zoologists, but one piece of wood: the winning post of the Epsom Derby."[26]

A North American champion at two and three, Nasrullah's son Nashua set a career earnings record on the racetrack and was purchased for an unprecedented $1,251,200 after his retirement from racing. (Keeneland Library)

Chapter 6

An Unlikely Horseman

On November 27, 1950, John A. Bell III and his wife returned home to their leased property at Hamburg Place outside Lexington. They were coming from Knoxville, Tennessee, where they had watched the Kentucky Wildcats football team eke out a one-point victory over their archrivals, the Tennessee Volunteers. What was normally a four-hour car trip took much longer that day, as the couple encountered an unusual early-season snowstorm that left the bluegrass blanketed in knee-deep snow. The following day Bell received a phone call from Lexington's Southern Railway station, letting him know that six of Robert Sterling Clark's mares had arrived. One of the mares was Singing Grass, in foal to Nasrullah. The area roads were still covered with snow and ice, and Bell was not relishing the prospect of transporting Clark's valuable stock before conditions improved. Bell's request that the mares be allowed to remain on the railcars for the night was denied, so he quickly thought of an alternative scheme. He arranged for stalls to be prepared for the mares at Lexington's Standardbred racetrack and found grooms to walk the horses through the snow to their temporary lodging, fortunately less than a half mile from the station. The hardy bunch of mares had already endured a hurricane at sea during their transatlantic trip from Southampton, England, to New York City. But they made it to their stalls at the trotting track without incident, where they would remain for several days until the roads became safe for van travel.[1]

On March 26, 1951, Bell and his wife attended a memorial dinner honoring the late head of the University of Kentucky's animal husbandry department. Upon returning to the farm around 11:30, Bell went straight to the foaling barn, where he found Singing Grass and her newborn chestnut colt. The mare and foal were exhausted, as was Andy Curd, the foreman who had helped the undersized mare deliver her unusually large colt. The newborn colt was having difficulty breathing, and his right foreleg was tucked awkwardly under his body, a result of the difficult delivery. Bell was concerned about the colt's chances for survival and retrieved a bottle of bourbon whiskey from a desk in the barn office. After a quick slug for himself, he poured some of the bottle's contents down the throat of the struggling foal and rubbed the spillage around its nose. The elixir revived the woozy colt, which would fittingly be named Never Say Die. Though Bell had been working with horses professionally for only a few years, he had grown up around all sorts of animals on his family's farm. But his childhood was hardly that of a typical early-twentieth-century farm boy.[2]

Bell was born in 1918 and raised on his family's suburban Pittsburgh compound. His grandfather, John Arner Bell Sr., had amassed a sizable fortune in banking and mining, making him one of Pittsburgh's wealthiest and most influential citizens at a time when the city was a manufacturing juggernaut and a major financial center. Situated at the confluence of the Allegheny and Monongahela Rivers, where they form the headwaters of the mighty Ohio, Pittsburgh had been a strategic location in pre-European times before being "discovered" by French explorer Robert de La Salle in the mid-seventeenth century. The French and British fought for control of the area in the French and Indian War, with the British emerging victorious. The British built

Hamburg Place foaling barn, the site of Never Say Die's 1951 birth.

Fort Pitt where the French Fort Duquesne had been, and they established the settlement of Pittsborough (as it was first called) on the same site. Both the fort and the town were named after William Pitt, the British secretary of state (and later prime minister) in charge of the American colonies, who was credited with turning the tide and helping the British achieve victory over the French.

Pittsburgh (as the town was officially known after 1794) grew slowly along with the young American nation, and it was the site of an early manufacturing industry in the face of international trade restrictions during the War of 1812. During the Civil War, Pittsburgh was an important armaments supplier. But it would not be until after the war that Pittsburgh's signature industry—steel—would help make the city one of the most important industrial centers in the United States and the world. The city's proximity to a major river and the coalfields of western Pennsylvania and West Virginia made it an ideal location to produce the material that would play such a prominent role in the construction of the modernizing world, including railroad tracks and skyscrapers. In the late nineteenth century a Scottish immigrant named Andrew Carnegie made one of the largest fortunes in the history of civilization with his Pittsburgh steel business.[3]

By the time of John A. Bell III's birth in 1918, Pittsburgh's leading corporate citizens included U.S. Steel, Alcoa, Gulf Oil, Westinghouse, and Heinz, as well as Andrew Mellon's various financial institutions. The estate on which Bell's family lived in Carnegie, Pennsylvania, contained houses for chauffeurs, gardeners, and other staff, including the caretaker of a kennel of prized Irish terriers. Bell's grandfather lived in the big house, and Bell's family and his aunt had smaller houses within the compound. In addition to the residential estate, Bell's grandfather owned a thousand-acre dairy farm called Bell Farm in nearby Coraopolis. The farm had some of the finest Holstein cows in the country and supplied milk to Pittsburgh hospitals, hotels, and restaurants with an on-site bottling operation. In addition to the herd raised for its milk, the farm was home to a collection of show animals, including cows, sheep, and horses. The farm's herd of show cattle rivaled that of Carnation and Pabst as one of the best in the nation. As an eight-year-old, John A. Bell III showed the grand champion cow at the New York State Fair against professional showmen. Eight teams of Clydesdale horses did the farmwork, but as a child Bell had his own team of ponies and wagons to play with.

Bell spent his childhood summers on the farm, playing alongside the workers and assisting them in their duties as best he could. There, Bell developed a love of animals and received a hands-on introduction to animal husbandry. But before he finished elementary school, Bell's grandfather was forced to sell the compound; the family moved to the dairy farm for a while but soon lost that as well. The circumstances surrounding the downfall of his grandfather would remain a mystery to Bell until he reached adulthood. While in the army during World War II, Bell met a stranger from Pittsburgh in the bar car on a cross-country train ride. That stranger gave Bell his first introduction to his grandfather's fascinating rise and fall of Shakespearean proportions.

John A. Bell Sr.'s climb from humble beginnings to wealth and power could have been taken straight from the pages of a nineteenth-century Horatio Alger novel. He started his professional life as a grocery store clerk, saved some money over time, and purchased a small flour mill, which he operated until his early thirties. Many Gilded Age paths to wealth and prominence passed through smoky taverns and back rooms where political maneuvering was lubricated with cigars, whiskey, and handshakes. Bell's path was no different.

In 1888 he was elected Allegheny County treasurer, which introduced him to the intersection of the worlds of finance and politics. After two three-year terms in the treasurer's office, which included a lawsuit Bell filed against the county over a salary dispute, he landed a job with the Freehold National Bank and eventually became its president (the bank would later be acquired by Colonial Trust Company). He then formed the Carnegie Trust Company (named after the Pittsburgh suburb of Carnegie) and served as that company's president. Later he served in the same capacity for a handful of other financial institutions, including the First National Bank of Carnegie, the Grove City National Bank, and the Burgettstown National Bank.

In the mining world, Bell consolidated five companies into the Carnegie Coal Company, a $20 million corporation whose stock Bell later controlled in its entirety, according to his *New York Times* obituary. Along with the mines themselves, Bell owned various company towns and bank branches that serviced them. It would be the dangerous mixture of banking and coal operations that eventually led to his downfall in the wake of a downturn in the volatile coal market. Bell was also involved in oil and real estate ventures in the United States, Colombia, Ecuador, and Venezuela and was a director of Sinclair Oil Company. At the peak of his wealth, power, and influence in the early 1920s, Bell's personal fortune was estimated to be as high as $25 million, and he employed thousands of workers in his mines, banks, and other concerns. He was active in the Pennsylvania Republican political machine and appeared primed to make a jump to the U.S. Senate.

In 1921 Pennsylvania senator Philander Knox died in office, and Governor William C. Sproul appointed William E. Crow to fill the seat until the next scheduled election the following year. Bell was considered a leading candidate for the Republican nomination early in 1922, but scandalous accusations flooded the Pennsylvania political scene that would eventually kill Bell's senatorial ambitions. With interim senator Crow gravely ill in March 1922, allegations of a deal between Bell and Crow were leaked to the press. According to the unsubstantiated rumors, Bell had offered Crow $650,000 (a sum that would have allowed Crow to repay some substantial debts before he died) to resign from office. Implicit in the allegations was the belief that Governor Sproul would appoint Bell to fill the vacant seat before the election, allowing Bell to run in the May primaries as the incumbent Republican senator—an almost invincible position in Pennsylvania at the time.

Bell vehemently denied the allegations. "I will make no settlement with anyone in return for a seat in the United States Senate," he declared. "There has been no such settlement by me; there never will be, and I will not have anything to do with any such arrangement. If you can find stronger language in which to state my position, use it." The governor was similarly indignant. "Mr. Bell is not the kind of man who would enter into such a deal as those almost infamous reports speak of," said Sproul. "He is a man of the highest character, who has lived an honorable life as a Christian gentleman. I have made no promises to any one respecting an appointment to the Senate."[4]

No one denounced the alleged corrupt bargain in stronger

terms than Senator Crow. "Within the past twenty-four hours
there has been published a slanderous and uncalled for report of
my probable resignation from the United States Senate, and the
probable appointment of Mr. John A. Bell to the vacancy, and the
candidacy of Mr. Bell for the full term," Crow declared. "This
wild, weird and lying report is so absurd on its face that a mere
denial hardly seems enough. For Mr. John A. Bell, the very soul
of honor, integrity and patriotism, to be made a victim of so vile
a conspiracy of slander and defamation is to my mind the most
serious feature of the case. As for myself, I rarely attempt to run
down political lies, and I am branding this so-called 'deal' on the
Senatorship as an infamous lie, lest silence on my part might be
misunderstood."[5]

Less than two weeks after news of the alleged scandal broke,
Bell was out of the race. Bell's exit and Crow's confirmation that
he would not seek reelection left David A. Reed, a World War I
veteran and Pittsburgh lawyer, as the lone candidate. Reed had
met with Secretary of the Treasury Andrew Mellon in Washington, D.C., days after reports of the alleged Bell-Crow deal
surfaced. In the aftermath of the 1921 deaths of both of Pennsylvania's U.S. senators—Philander Knox and Boise Penrose—Mellon was as influential a figure in Republican politics as any, and
his approval of Reed as a Senate candidate was an extremely important endorsement.

The historical record does not reveal whether Mellon's support of Reed reflected any personal animosity toward Bell or
simply a desire to rid the party of the stench of scandal. The
fact that Reed was the son of Mellon's friend and business associate certainly could not have hurt the young politician. Given
that Mellon and Bell were contemporaries and competitors in the
Pittsburgh business community, the two were certainly familiar
with each other, but they were not close friends. Mellon was one
of the wealthiest and most influential men in the United States,
and his endorsement of Reed all but killed any other candidacy.

Though the end of his senatorial ambitions was a difficult experience to endure, things were about to become much worse for Bell. Coal prices, which had soared during World War I and its immediate aftermath, collapsed in the 1920s. Bell struggled to meet payrolls at his various mines, and his problems quickly spread to his banking interests.

On April 27, 1925, Pennsylvania's secretary of banking issued a statement explaining the state's decision to close the Carnegie Trust Company, which Bell controlled:

> The reserve fund of the Carnegie Trust Company has been below the legal requirements for some days. Although every effort has been made by the company to build up the reserve fund to the required amount, it has failed to do so. Owing to the frozen condition of its assets, which in turn is a direct result of the stagnation that has [occurred] in the bituminous coal industry of Pennsylvania for some months, the trust company is the holder of obligations of coal companies aggregating a considerable sum. Because of these conditions it was my duty as the Secretary of Banking to take possession of the business and property of the trust company in order that the interests of the depositors and other creditors might be protected.[6]

Another Bell-controlled bank, the First National Bank of Carnegie (located across the street from the shuttered bank), was also forced to close its doors fifteen minutes after opening that day due to the long lines formed by concerned depositors. Bell issued a statement to reassure the customers: "The First National Bank of Carnegie is in fine shape and will be reopened but I cannot say when."[7]

The *New York Times* expressed guarded confidence that the problems associated with Bell's banks might soon be resolved. "Mr. Bell is declared to be a victim of the fact that the bottom has fallen out of the bituminous coal industry, in which his holdings are large. His financial difficulties—extending a year or more—have been the subject of study by some of the biggest financial and business persons of the country, including Secretary Mellon and Harry F. Sinclair, the oil man. A group of bankers met [in Pittsburgh] late today and appeared confident of saving Bell."[8] But soon allegations of misdeeds and misappropriations by Bell and others came to light, and Bell declared bankruptcy. At that point, any discussions of what would today be referred to as a "bailout" quickly dried up.

On August 4, 1925, Bell was charged with twelve counts of embezzlement, involving more than $800,000 of false bank entries, and two counts of lying to Pennsylvania Banking Department officials about the condition of his Carnegie Trust Company. Facing up to seventy years in prison, he was convicted and sentenced to six and a half.[9] The defense moved to have the sentence stayed in light of the fact that Bell was now partially paralyzed as a result of three strokes he had suffered since his indictment, but the motion was denied. Bell served two years of the sentence in a hospital. After being granted parole in 1929, at age seventy-five, Bell expressed his intention of "making good and paying back every cent I owe," but he died less than four years later, having spent most of his final days incapacitated in a Pennsylvania sanitarium.[10] Among those at Bell Sr.'s funeral was a large contingent of coal miners who wanted to show their appreciation for Bell's efforts on their behalf under trying circumstances.

At the time of John A. Bell Sr.'s death, the family was left virtually penniless. John A. Bell Jr. had lost most of his assets in conjunction with his father's bankruptcy. The farm survived for a couple of years on the proceeds from milk sales, but it was eventually sold to pay off some of the debt created by the bank failure, and that land is now occupied by the Pittsburgh International Airport.

After his grandfather's death, Bell III moved with his mother and siblings to his maternal grandmother's house in Auburn,

New York, where her family manufactured furniture. Bell's father utilized some of his significant business contacts, forged over the course of his father's career, and established Southwest Supply Company in Tulsa, Oklahoma, which supplied line pipe, drill pipe, and other drilling equipment to oil companies. His partner in the venture was John Phillips, son of the founder of Phillips Petroleum Company, which became Southwest Supply's largest customer.

John Phillips had worked for his father's company and had even served on its board of directors until his father, Frank Phillips, finally lost patience with his ne'er-do-well son. Frank reached his breaking point when John spectacularly failed to carry out a seemingly simple assignment. Frank had sent John to Kansas City to meet with some of the company's eastern directors and then bring them back to Phillips headquarters in Oklahoma. But upon arrival in Kansas City, John, who was known to overindulge in alcohol, embarked on an evening of drinking. At the last bar of the night, John encountered a bartender in possession of a spider monkey, which John negotiated to buy. The next morning John forgot about his scheduled meeting but made it back to the train station to board his father's private car, which was waiting to take John and the directors back to Oklahoma. Company executives and employees were assembled at the Bartlesville, Oklahoma, train station to greet the important out-of-town guests. A band had even been hired for the occasion. But the music stopped when only John and his spider monkey emerged from the train and it became apparent that John was unaccompanied by the men he had been assigned to deliver. John Phillips was soon completely disassociated from Phillips Petroleum, but his contacts in the industry were invaluable for Southwest Supply Company. That company made enough money for John Bell Jr. to move his family back to suburban Pittsburgh, where he bought a farm in Sewickley Heights that he named "Jonabell."

Like his son, Bell Jr. loved animals. He had shown his Irish terriers in dog shows as a young man, including a trip to the Westminster show at New York City's Madison Square Garden. At Jonabell Farm he reestablished a herd of Holstein cows, though on a much smaller scale than at his father's Bell Farm. Additionally, on the advice of his veterinarian, he acquired a few Thoroughbred mares. He also brought in a Thoroughbred stallion through the U.S. Army's Remount program, which was designed to ensure a supply of cavalry horses for military purposes.[11] Bell quickly realized that breeding second-rate mares to military-issue stallions was not the way to create an economically viable equine operation, and he sought expert advice to help him chart a new course.

Bell was put in touch with a Thoroughbred bloodstock adviser in Kentucky named Tom Cromwell, who advised Bell to sell his stock at an upcoming sale in Lexington. He further recommended that if Bell was serious about starting an equine program, he should attend the annual yearling sales in Saratoga, New York, and purchase well-bred fillies to race and to keep as broodmares after their track careers were over. Bell took Cromwell's advice and met him in Saratoga in 1939, where the pair picked out a chestnut filly from the first crop of Alfred Gwynne Vanderbilt's top runner Discovery, purchasing the filly for $750 at auction.[12] Cromwell introduced Bell to trainer Max Hirsch, who inspected the filly and said he would be glad to train her.

Born in Fredericksburg, Texas, in 1880, Hirsch was the grandson of a German immigrant and the son of a Union Army veteran who supported his six children as the town postmaster. Max worked from a young age on a nearby ranch owned by John Morris, who was heavily involved in eastern racing as a stable owner and racetrack operator. At the age of ten, Hirsch began riding horses in local races. Two years later, while helping to load a string of horses on a train bound for Baltimore, he made the fateful decision to climb aboard without alerting his family or anyone else. "It was a hot day, and I was barefooted," Hirsch

The trainer of three Kentucky Derby winners, Hall of Famer Max Hirsch (left) gave John A. Bell III his start in the Thoroughbred business by entrusting him with a string of yearlings to break in 1946. (Keeneland Library)

would later recall. "Suddenly the urge hit me. I had to go with the horses. So, clad in blue jeans and without a word to my parents, I climbed aboard a freight car with the horses and was off to Baltimore."[13]

He found a job working for a trainer on the East Coast and in 1895 won his first race as a professional rider for the Morris family, launching a brief career that included 123 wins in 1,117 starts. But Hirsch soon grew too large to be a jockey and turned to training because "there was nothing else I could do to make a dollar. All of my life had been spent around horses."[14] He won his first race as a trainer in New Orleans in 1905, but the early years were lean ones. He had his first starter in the Kentucky Derby in 1915, the year Regret became the first filly to win Kentucky's great race, but more hard times followed for Hirsch. "Tough sledding. Chicken today, feathers the rest of the week," Hirsch later recalled.[15]

Hirsch's big break came when he purchased Grey Lag from the "Wizard of the Turf," John E. Madden, as a yearling in 1919. As a two-year-old, the colt was slow to develop, but he showed enough promise that leading trainer Sam Hildreth approached Hirsch on behalf of oil tycoon Harry F. Sinclair, who had recently purchased Rancocas Farm (the previous owner had been tobacco manufacturer Pierre Lorillard IV, the first American to win the English Derby in 1881). Hirsch told Hildreth that the colt could be had for $40,000, but the superstitious Hildreth nixed the deal after discovering a mysterious patch of gray hair hidden under the horse's saddlecloth. Days later, Grey Lag won the Champagne Stakes, one of New York's most important races for two-year-olds. Prior to the race, Sinclair had lamented to Hirsch that he had been experiencing a run of poor betting luck. This prompted the trainer to give Sinclair a tip: Grey Lag to win. After the race, with his bad luck ended, Sinclair approached Hirsch to inquire about purchasing the colt. By that time, Hirsch's asking price had jumped to $60,000, which Sinclair quickly accepted, gray hairs and all.[16]

Hirsch made a national name for himself as the trainer of the great gelding Sarazen, the top racehorse in America in 1924 and 1925. Sarazen was sold as a two-year-old by Colonel Phil T. Chinn to Virginia Fair Vanderbilt, heir to her father's Comstock Lode fortune and wife of William Kissam Vanderbilt II (himself an early adviser to the Aga Khan in matters of horse racing). Hirsch soon began to attract a variety of top American owners, including, most famously, the King Ranch Stable, and won his first of three Kentucky Derbies in 1936 with Bold Venture.

The filly that Hirsch agreed to train for Bell Jr. in 1939 would be named Dark Discovery. She was sent from New York to Hartland Farm outside Versailles, Kentucky, to be taught to carry a rider that fall; then she was sent to Hirsch's winter quarters at the State Fair Grounds in Columbia, South Carolina, to begin training. Dark Discovery was the second-best three-year-old filly of her generation and gave the Bell family an exciting introduction to the sport of horse racing.

At the 1941 Coaching Club American Oaks, Dark Discovery just missed catching the front-running Level Best (the eventual three-year-old champion filly) at the wire. Two weeks later, John Bell III graduated with honors from Princeton with a degree in geology. To his schoolmates at Princeton, Bell was known as "Pappy," a shortened version of the name "Father Time," which referred to Bell's deliberate gait and speech. Though he was an articulate speaker and capable athlete, he always maintained a methodical and unhurried demeanor. He had majored in geology with a vague intention of entering the mining business (or at least with a halfhearted desire to preserve that option). That September he enrolled in business school at Harvard, which offered an accelerated one-year program to prepare students for the burgeoning world of war industries. But the Japanese attack on Pearl Harbor in December brought the United States fully into World War II. Bell was drafted into the Army Administrative Medical Corps and served from 1942 until 1946, achieving the rank of second lieutenant.

Upon leaving the army, Bell had little professional direction. He was told that his bachelor's degree in geology was of little use in the "real world" and that he would need to pursue graduate study to catch up with the technological advances in the field. His only job offer in oil or mining would have required relocation to Venezuela, which did not interest him. Bell's father told him to take some time to figure things out and, fortuitously, sent Bell III down to Lexington to check on some mares he kept there for breeding purposes as part of his growing equine operation. Bell managed to extend his stay by landing a job with prominent veterinarian Art Davidson; his duties entailed accompanying the vet on his rounds to bluegrass horse farms, opening gates, cleaning equipment, and holding horses.

The days were long, but Bell enjoyed the work and was happy to be out of Pittsburgh. He managed to have an active social life with the help of Miss Marnie Marr, who arranged a series of blind dates for Bell with a bevy of eligible young ladies, none of whom was to Bell's liking. On what was supposed to be his last night in Kentucky before returning to Pennsylvania, Bell attended a Saturday night dance at the Lexington Country Club with another blind date, and as with all the others, sparks failed to fly. Miss Marr was at the dance, and Bell reported to her, once again, that this girl was not his type. Marr asked, "Well, what in the hell is your type?" Bell spotted a tall young lady walking across the dance floor and pointed her out to Marr: "That is more my type." Marr promised to arrange a date with the woman if he could manage to extend his stay. Bell replied, "It's a deal." The woman in question was Jessica Gay, who had deep Kentucky ties. Her father was a central Kentucky farmer, and her mother had served as the ceremonial First Lady of Kentucky for her widower grandfather, Governor James Bennett McCreary, during his second stint in the governor's mansion.[17]

But John A. Bell III knew nothing about Jessica Gay's ancestors or their politics, and he would have cared little anyway. He was simply glad to get a date with an attractive young lady. Following graduation from the University of Kentucky with a degree in journalism, Gay had written news copy for WHAS in Louisville before moving to New York City. When she was introduced to Bell, Gay was back home contemplating her future after undergoing an appendectomy. Bell and Gay had a successful first date that included "lots of whiskey."[18] The couple was married in January 1947, and Bell's planned two-week visit to Lexington ended up lasting sixty years.

Still without professional direction, Bell and his new bride headed off on a cross-country honeymoon—an automobile trip

Assault, the "Clubfooted Comet," won the 1946 American Triple Crown for trainer Max Hirsch. (Courtesy of University of Kentucky Archives)

bound for Los Angeles. They took a northern route, passing through Montana, where Bell had spent time studying geology and working on a dude ranch during summer breaks from Princeton. They intended to return home via Route 66 from Los Angeles to Chicago, a highway famously referenced in the hit song "(Get Your Kicks on) Route 66," written by Bobby Troup, a high school friend and former bandmate of Bell's (who had played the saxophone in his youth), and recorded by Nat King Cole the previous year. The newlyweds' trip would be financed by a series of bets Bell had made the previous spring on American Triple Crown winner Assault, trained by Max Hirsch for the powerful Texas-based King Ranch Stables.

Assault was called the "Clubfooted Comet" by his admirers because of a deformity resulting from a wound incurred as a youngster when he stepped on a surveyor's stake. Though the injury prevented him from walking normally, the horse had no trouble at a full gallop. Assault won the Kentucky Derby by a whopping eight lengths, a Derby record, at odds of 8–1. One week later, Bell parlayed the proceeds of a winning Derby bet into a winning Preakness score when Assault opened up a wide lead in the stretch and just managed to hold off a charging Lord Boswell at the wire. Despite his victories in the first two Triple Crown races, some fans doubted Assault's ability to last the 1½-mile distance of the final leg, the Belmont Stakes, and bettors made the fast-finishing Lord Boswell the favorite. Bell's faith had not diminished, however, and he rolled his profits from Assault's first two victories into a bet on him to win the Belmont. When the colt came from behind to win the race and capture the American Triple Crown, Bell netted enough money to buy a Buick and finance a honeymoon.

But in an example of living and dying by the proverbial sword, the bankroll lasted only as far as Idaho, where a bad run at the gambling tables outside Sun Valley put the rest of the trip in jeopardy. The young couple had made no secret of their extended and extravagant itinerary, bragging to both friends and family, and they were reluctant to return home earlier than scheduled. So the honeymooners pushed on to Pasadena, California, where they found a cheap room and extended their trip with some successful handicapping and wagering at nearby Santa Anita racetrack.

Back in Kentucky after the honeymoon adventure, Bell initially returned to his position as a veterinary assistant. But soon his lack of professional direction was resolved by none other than trainer Max Hirsch, who had purchased a string of yearling horses and needed someone to introduce them to the saddle and provide initial basic training, a process known as "breaking." The job was Bell's if he could find acceptable facilities. Hirsch even assured the young man that his inexperience was an asset

Hamburg Place, purchased by John E. Madden with proceeds from the sale of a horse named Hamburg, was the birthplace of five Kentucky Derby winners and Never Say Die. (Postcard courtesy of University of Kentucky Archives)

because he would be forced to follow the trainer's instructions exactly. With few other options available to him, Bell accepted Hirsch's offer and took a month-to-month lease on a sixteen-stall tobacco barn with two fenced fields on Georgetown Pike outside Lexington. He spent the fall working with the yearlings and delivered them safe, sound, and saddle-broken to Hirsch's winter headquarters in South Carolina.

Bell's work received good reviews from Hirsch, and when he returned to Lexington, Bell learned that one of the most successful and historically significant farms in the history of American horse racing was available to rent. After consulting with his father, who agreed to transfer his horses to his son's care, Bell arranged to rent roughly half of Hamburg Place. He and his wife moved from a Lexington duplex to a small tenant house on the farm. They were in the horse business, and they called the operation Jonabell Farm, after Bell's father's Pennsylvania acreage. This would be the birthplace of Never Say Die.

Hamburg Place had been founded in 1898 by John E. Madden, the legendary horse breeder, owner, trainer, and trader who had bred and raised Grey Lag, the horse that first brought Max Hirsch national recognition. Madden's spread was named after a horse he had sold as a two-year-old in 1897 for a reported $40,001 (a record at the time) to copper king Marcus Daley. This sale afforded Madden the opportunity to buy the farm, which had once been in the family of the wife of the "Great Compromiser" Henry Clay.[19] (The fact that the farm shared a name with the German port town that later played such an important role in the Beatles' rise to fame would be particularly fascinating to Beatles drummer Pete Best, who visited the farm many years later with John Bell III while touring with the Pete Best Band.)

When Madden originally purchased the land, the farm was an easy ride on horseback from downtown Lexington. "I wanted a place near town," Madden recalled, "so if I had a customer, I could get him out there before he changed his mind."[20] Madden initially purchased 235 acres of what had been known as Overton Farm, but he continued to expand until it totaled more than 2,000 acres.

Madden was born in 1856 in Bethlehem, Pennsylvania, to immigrants from Roscommon, Ireland. Madden's father died in 1860, leaving his wife to care for five children. Madden was a prodigious athlete, owning local running records at distances ranging from 100 yards to 5 miles; he was also captain of his baseball team and was even an amateur boxing champion. He was introduced to the world of horse racing as a driver of trotting horses on the Pennsylvania state fair circuit. He soon bought his first horse and started training, but he never missed an opportunity to compete in footraces or boxing matches. He learned the art of buying, selling, and trading horses on the trotting scene and developed a maxim that would serve him well throughout his career: "Better to sell and repent than to keep and repent."[21]

At the age of thirty, Madden came to Kentucky, taking a

Known as the "Wizard of the Turf," John E. Madden (right foreground) was among the most influential American horsemen in history. (Keeneland Library)

suite of rooms in Lexington's Phoenix Hotel, the top gathering place for locals and out-of-towners interested in horse talk, deals, rumor, and gossip. "When I left Bethlehem, Pennsylvania," Madden later recalled, "my chief stock in trade was pride and a few good trotting horses."[22] Gradually, Madden switched his focus from trotters to Thoroughbreds, and in 1898 he won the Kentucky Derby with a horse he had bought the previous year named Plaudit. He would go on to breed five more Kentucky Derby winners at his Hamburg Place, including the first American Triple Crown winner, Sir Barton.

There was no shrewder horse trader in his day than Madden, and his strict rules of horsemanship, which he posted in every barn, established an industry-wide standard. His success as an owner, trainer, gambler, breeder, and trader of racehorses was unmatched in all of American racing in the early twentieth century (and, arguably, at any time before or since).[23] Madden demanded nothing short of excellence from his staff, strictly regulating their language, dress, and demeanor, in addition to requiring adherence to the highest standards of horsemanship and attention to detail. He famously stipulated, "Coca-Cola addicts need not apply" for any job opening at Hamburg Place.

From 1898 to 1929, Madden bred an astonishing 182 stakes winners, but by the late 1920s, he had almost completely abandoned the horse business, preferring to spend his time and money on Wall Street.[24] In October 1929 he detected the onset of a cold as he left his Wall Street offices and returned to his suite at the Pennsylvania Hotel on a particularly cool and damp evening. The man who had made a habit of taking a daily swim in the Hamburg Place pond regardless of the season, who preferred leaping over fences to opening gates until late in life, and who claimed to have never been sick a day in his life quickly developed pneumonia. He refused to be admitted to a hospital, however, and would leap out of bed to shadowbox with visitors to demonstrate that he was on the mend. He sent his son, who had traveled from Oklahoma to see him, back to Hamburg Place to attend to some affairs, and Madden died alone in his hotel room of a heart attack.

To his disappointment, Madden's two sons did not share their father's love for the sport of horse racing. His younger son, Joseph, took his own life in a New York City department store in 1932, at which time his older son, Edward, purchased most of his brother's inherited share of Hamburg Place and moved back to the farm, where he raised a few polo ponies. Sadly, Edward's life was also cut short by a self-inflicted gunshot wound. Following Edward's death, the surviving Madden heirs needed to generate some income from the farm, so they sought a renter and found one in John A. Bell III.

It was on the farm made famous by the Wizard of the Turf that Never Say Die was born in March 1951. After barely surviving birth, Never Say Die made marked improvement at his

John A. Bell III with a horse. Bell administered a timely dose of whiskey to a newborn Never Say Die, helping him survive a difficult birth. (Courtesy of Bennett Bell Williams)

mother's side in the same fields that had served as a nursery for five Kentucky Derby winners. In January of Never Say Die's yearling year, Bell wrote to Sterling Clark to describe the colt's progress. "This fellow has been the most surprising and pleasing development of all," Bell reported. "He has improved beyond belief and I'll guarantee that you wouldn't recognize him. He is growing into a very powerful, well-proportioned yearling. The only defect that I see in him at the moment is that he wings out in the right foot. This leg was always crooked, but it is improving greatly with time. Knowing the blood that is in this colt, he might be a real good one."[25]

In May, Bell gave Clark another update: "This colt is doing fine in every respect except that he is extremely studdish. If he gets much worse, I will be forced to put him in a paddock by himself. However I am very much against putting them in sep-

Never Say Die was raised in the same Hamburg Place fields that produced scores of stakes winners for John E. Madden. (Postcard courtesy of University of Kentucky Archives)

arate paddocks because that treatment invariably makes them more studdish. He is getting plenty of kicks and bites from his playmates, and I am hoping they will put him on a more even keel. The colt is developing wonderfully well and will undoubtedly be a big, strong, powerful horse. He is not too pleasing to the eye, but I think he will grow more so as he gets older."[26]

A month later, Bell reported to Clark, "I can't quite make up my mind whether I really like this colt or don't. I don't imagine we will get too much answer until he actually faces the barrier. He ought to be big enough, and tough enough to take a whole lot of training and I would guess that he would be quite durable." As Bell would later recall, Never Say Die continued his bullying ways in the paddocks with the other young colts "until one day [another] colt tied into him pretty good and gave him a good licking. He was pretty well whipped, and it made a different fellow of him. We never had any more trouble, and when breaking time came he did everything we asked."[27]

John A. Bell III (left) with yearlings. Bell oversaw the breaking of Never Say Die before the horse was sent to England for his racing career. (Courtesy of Bennett Bell Williams)

Prior to 1951, Clark typically sent all his young horses back to his Sundridge Farm in Virginia for weaning. But Bell had convinced Clark to leave four mares and foals, including Never Say Die, in Kentucky for weaning and breaking. Never Say Die was taught to carry a rider by Bell and his team, a gradual process that can take weeks; it begins with the horse being introduced to bridle and saddle in an enclosed area and concludes with horse and rider working together in an open field. In his final review of Clark's stock, Bell wrote to the owner, "I would think now that you are certain to have one top prospect out of the four, but I'd hate to try to pick out the one to do the running. Certainly any trainer should be glad to get the four of them."[28] Upon completion of his basic education, Never Say Die was sent to Clark's farm in Virginia before being shipped to England to begin his final preparation for the races under the tutelage of veteran trainer Joseph Lawson, who was indeed glad to have him.[29]

Chapter 7

A Derby-less Trainer

Upon arrival in England, Never Say Die was sent to Carlburg Stables, the Newmarket training yard of seventy-two-year-old Joe Lawson. At that time, Sterling Clark split his horses between Lawson and another trainer named Harry Peacock. Peacock had won a coin flip to determine which man would receive first choice of Clark's horses that year. Though he liked the look of Never Say Die, Peacock was not interested in training a son of Nasrullah. Nasrullah was well on his way to having one of the most outstanding stud careers in history, but the memory of the stallion's inability to reach his potential because of his idiosyncrasies was still fresh in the minds of many horsemen. Peacock's lack of faith in Nasrullah's offspring was Lawson's gain and would bring the veteran trainer one last taste of celebrity in the waning years of a lengthy and accomplished career.

Born in the northeast of England in 1881, near where the River Tyne flows into the North Sea, Lawson had grown up, like so many trainers, with an ambition to be a jockey. But by the age of sixteen he was already battling to make weight and had to give up the trade. He signed on at the famous Manton training yard in 1898, where he would spend close to half a century, eventually taking over as master trainer. His boss for the first thirty years at Manton was "Young" Alec Taylor, who, along with his half brother Tom, had inherited Manton from their father in 1895. "Old" Alec Taylor had built the state-of-the-art facility with the help of a wealthy owner and some successful betting coups. They selected the location outside of Marlborough in Wiltshire, on the main road from London to Bath, for its seclusion from crowds, touts, and bookmakers' spies. The yard was practically perfect when Taylor began training there in 1870. The *Sporting Life* reported, "Those fortunate enough to visit the Manton establishment cannot fail to be impressed by the completeness of every detail. The buildings possess a singularly attractive and quiet beauty. [There are] spacious paddocks, splendid stables, and boxes [stalls] unsurpassed for size and abundance of light and air."[1] Old Taylor trained the winners of eight classics at Manton, laying the foundation for its reputation as one of the most famous and prestigious training facilities in all of Britain.

Initially, Alec and Tom struggled to duplicate their father's success at Manton. Alec had served under his father his entire working life and handled the training, while Tom controlled the business side of the operation. The brothers' fortunes worsened when a fifteen-year-old stable boy who had been in the Taylors' employ for only three months was admitted to a local hospital with signs of tubercular meningitis. The boy eventually died from the ailment, but not before authorities were alerted to severe bruising up and down his legs. Newspapers began to investigate rumors of abuse suffered by young employees at the hands of Manton managers, and the National Society for the Prevention of Cruelty to Children quickly gave its support to the investigation. Former stable hands came out of the proverbial woodwork to tell tales of corporal punishment meted out at the famous training yard. Tom Taylor and two other foremen were consistently identified as the primary offenders. The three men were charged with manslaughter and "assault causing grievous bodily harm" in the case of the young stable boy, but when the coroner concluded that the cause of his death was meningitis, the manslaughter charges were dropped. Tom Taylor was subsequently acquitted of the assault charge because of insufficient evidence of the severity of the beatings and the existence of the Master and Servant Act, which allowed masters to physically discipline their servants. The same defense was not available to the foremen, however, and they were both found guilty of assault.

The judge had choice words for the guilty parties: "The suggestion that a boy was somewhat late in the morning, or that the hot water in the afternoon was not as hot as it ought to be [is] no justification for any man taking a horse whip and a big stick and knocking a boy about." The judge then turned his wrath to the entire Manton operation: "I can only picture to myself [what] we have all read [about] the unfortunate and unhappy way [in] which the negroes lived in America before they were emancipated," he declared. "The life of this boy seems to have been that of a slave, as far as you were concerned."[2]

Though Tom Taylor had been acquitted, his reputation could not survive this public rebuke. In the court of public opinion, Tom was guilty of a child's murder. In the aftermath of the scandal, Alec and Tom dissolved their partnership. Alec, who had not been implicated in the beatings, pressed on as the owner and master trainer of Manton. Years later, a former employee of Old Taylor recalled that breakfast at Manton had consisted of tea, bread, and cuts from a riding crop, with the only second helpings coming from the crop.[3] But with Tom's departure and Alec's ascension to complete control of the operation, those days were gone forever.

Young Alec Taylor won some well-needed favorable publicity for himself and his operation when one of the greatest fillies in the history of racing, Sceptre, landed in his barn. As a yearling, the impeccably bred Sceptre (her sire was a Derby winner and her dam was a full sister to a Triple Crown winner) was included in the dispersal sale of her breeder, the Duke of Westminster, conducted by the leading British auction house Tattersalls.

The late duke's heir hoped to purchase the filly and keep her for the Westminster stable, but an eccentric and notorious character named Robert Sievier had also set his sights on Sceptre. By the age of forty, Sievier already had two failed marriages and a string of bankruptcies. He was living with a woman he was rumored to have "stolen" from her husband. Sievier was a racing journalist but was widely known as a wildly irresponsible gambler. As such, there were questions about his trustworthiness and his credit prior to the sale. The day before Sceptre was to be sold, Sievier approached the auctioneer with £20,000 in £500 notes (a figure equivalent to more than $2 million today), demanding recognition that his credit was good. The following day, Sievier was the successful bidder for Sceptre, who fetched a price of 10,000 guineas, a record for a yearling that would stand for two decades.

After she won two of three races as a two-year-old, her first trainer accepted an offer to work privately for a different owner, so Sievier bought a training yard and prepared Sceptre himself for the classics. She won four of the five English classics as well as the St. James's Palace Stakes and the Nassau Stakes in a remarkable three-year-old season. The one classic she failed to win was the Derby, which cost Sievier a sizable bet.

Sievier brought Sceptre to Tattersalls to be sold in December, but she looked disheveled and exhausted and did not reach her reserve price of 25,000 guineas. So Sievier decided to bring her back for one more race the following spring—the Lincolnshire Handicap, the first major event of the British racing season. Sceptre lost, but Sievier found a buyer in Sir William Bass, of the famous brewing family. Bass's father had owned horses with Old Alec Taylor, and he continued his family's allegiance to Manton by transferring Sceptre to Young Alec's barn. Sceptre returned to her winning ways for Taylor, capturing four more stakes in her two years under his care and bringing Taylor and the training yard some positive recognition after such a public lambasting.

The year after Sceptre's retirement, Taylor achieved success at the top level of English racing with a colt named Challacombe, which won the St. Leger in 1905—the first of Taylor's twenty-one career classic wins. Challacombe's owner was none other than Washington Singer, one of Isaac Merritt Singer's two dozen acknowledged children. Washington Singer had grown up in Oldway Mansion, the 115-room behemoth on the Devon coast of England that Singer had built with Washington's mother, Isabella, after being shunned by New York society. Washington Singer had found his way into the elite circles of the British turf and would eventually be elected into the ultraexclusive English Jockey Club—one of the first Americans so honored and one of the first members whose fortune was based in manufacturing.

Washington Singer's membership in the English Jockey Club was evidence that he had achieved a social status his father never could. It was also evidence that English high society was slowly adapting to the fact that new sources of wealth and power were shaping the modern world and the sport of horse racing. Jockey Club members had historically been selected from the ranks of the landed aristocracy, but in the early twentieth century, industrial magnates and their heirs were beginning to exert their influence on racing in a way that would permanently alter the sport's landscape.

With the help of Sceptre and Challacombe, Taylor had managed to return Manton to a position at the top of British racing, where his father had left it. In 1918 Taylor became the first (and, to date, only) trainer to win back-to-back English Triple Crowns when Lady James Douglas's colt Gainsborough captured the Two Thousand Guineas, the Derby, and St. Leger, duplicating the feat of Gay Crusader the previous year. To illustrate the remarkable run of success enjoyed by Taylor (and his crack team of employees, which included Joe Lawson), a Taylor-trained stallion named Bayardo was the sire of both Gainsborough and Gay Crusader.

Despite a string of top runners and leading-trainer titles,

Taylor was concerned about the future as World War I was drawing to a close on the Continent. Two of his top owners had left the sport, and Taylor was looking for financial security. Over the years, Taylor had made a habit of acquiring acreage adjacent to Manton whenever it came up for sale, and he had redoubled those efforts during the Great War, when real estate values were depressed. Following the war, land prices soared, and Taylor was ready to cash in. In early 1919 he announced that the entire spread (more than 5,000 acres) would be auctioned in September if a suitable offer were not accepted first.

Taylor found a buyer in Joseph Watson, who had made a sizable fortune when he sold his family's Leeds-based soap company to Lever Brothers, one of the largest businesses in Britain. Watson's purchase offer was conditional: Taylor had to stay on at Manton as head trainer—a condition Taylor accepted. The two made a formidable pair at the auction ring as Taylor selected top stock for Watson to buy, and they had early success on the racecourse as well.[4] But in 1922, just months after being granted the title Baron of Manton for his service during World War I, Watson suffered a fatal heart attack while on a Warwickshire foxhunt with his family.

The executors of Watson's estate decided that his children were too young to manage his racing affairs, so they dispersed his bloodstock and sought a buyer for Manton. In the meantime, the executors sold parcels of farmland to tenants, and Alec Taylor continued to preside over the still-successful training operation, with Joe Lawson as his faithful head assistant. Finally, in 1927, the executors found a buyer: Tattersalls had agreed to purchase the training yard. But Taylor's health was deteriorating, and the executors announced that the "Wizard of Manton" would be retiring at the end of the season, although he would continue to serve in an advisory capacity.

In a generation full of legendary horseman, Taylor was arguably the best, and his legacy would live on through his top assistant. The new owners named Joe Lawson, who had worked his way up from the bottom in three decades at the facility, as the new master of Manton. Lawson continued where Taylor left off, winning his first English classic in his second season with Waldorf Astor's filly Pennycomequick. Two years later, Lawson would break the record for annual purse money won by a trainer when his horses earned more than £93,000 (more than $5 million in modern U.S. dollars). The old record had stood for forty-two years before Lawson broke it, and his record would stand for twenty-six more. It was the victory of Washington Singer's talented two-year-old colt Orwell in the Imperial Produce Stakes that put Lawson over the top and into the record books.

Orwell began the following year, his three-year-old season, with an impressive victory in the Greenham Stakes at Newbury, and he quickly became an early favorite for the Derby. The colt justified the attention he was receiving with a victory in the first classic of the year, the Two Thousand Guineas. After that race, bookmakers were quoting odds as low as 2–1 on Orwell to win the Derby. As the big race drew near, rumors about a plot to poison the horse prompted Lawson and Singer to post two armed guards outside Orwell's stable. Despite questions about whether the colt was genetically inclined to last the Derby's 1½-mile distance, popular enthusiasm for Orwell was enormous. A huge crowd turned out at Epsom Downs; wild estimations of the crowd's size ran as high as a million. Whatever the actual number, the throng included the king and queen, as well as American flying sensation Amelia Earhart. Orwell became one of the heaviest favorites in years as morning odds of 15–8 shortened to 5–4 by race time. Punters lost an estimated $10 million on the colt, however, as he faded to finish ninth, proving that those who had doubted his stamina had been correct.

Lawson continued his successful run through the 1930s, winning another training title in 1936. In 1939 he won the One Thousand Guineas and the English Oaks with Robert Sterling

Clark's Galatea II, who was from the same maternal family as Never Say Die's dam, Singing Grass. But three months after Galatea's triumph in the Oaks, Germany invaded Poland, again sending Europe into full-scale war. Racing persevered during World War II, but it was conducted on a limited basis, and purses plummeted along with bloodstock values. Top stallions like the Aga Khan's Bahram and Mahmoud were sold to American interests to stand in the United States, where the equine industry was not suffering nearly as badly as it was in war-ravaged Europe. With tremendous wartime declines hitting the British equine industry, even the mighty Tattersalls struggled to survive.

By the time the Allies achieved victory in 1945, Tattersalls could no longer justify the expense of owning Manton and put the facility up for sale. Lawson told a local newspaper that he hoped to stay on: "I have been here 50 years and I don't want to leave. [If] the estate is sold and the new owner [asks] me to continue as trainer, I should be happy and willing to carry on. Otherwise I shall look for a [yard of] my own, as I have no intention of retiring."[5] When a buyer was found, Lawson was forced to leave the place he had called home for half a century. As promised, he searched for a yard of his own, but even in a soft postwar real estate market, he failed to find a suitable facility. At the age of sixty-six, he publicly contemplated retirement, leading *Sporting Life* to publish a story beneath the headline "Lawson to Retire."[6] But after a few months, he resumed his search for training space. He had won ten classics and dozens of other stakes races, but the Derby remained an elusive prize in an otherwise remarkable and complete career. He loved the challenge of developing equine athletes, but that one hole in his long list of professional accomplishments gave Lawson the incentive to continue training. After some deliberation, he decided to buy the Carlburg yard at Newmarket in Suffolk. And it was there, in late 1952, that Lawson welcomed the horse that would put a capstone on his distinguished career: Never Say Die.

Chapter 8

The First Kentucky-Bred Champion of the Epsom Derby

Never Say Die had been a large, spindly foal, but by the time he arrived at Newmarket, he had filled out to become a strapping young colt with a slightly better temperament than that of his notorious sire. Though he never displayed Nasrullah's mental peculiarities on the racetrack, Never Say Die did develop a reputation for moodiness and difficulty among the humans who cared for him. One British publication described Never Say Die as "a fine-looking chestnut, strong, tough and deep-bodied with powerful quarters and good limbs."[1] A turf writer for the *Daily Express* who called himself "The Scout" observed that Never Say Die had a coarse head and a Roman nose that the writer attributed to the presence of Man o' War in Never Say Die's pedigree; he attributed the horse's low-set tail to the influence of the Italian stallion Nearco. The Scout commented further, "He has an excellent, strong, straight pair of hind legs, even if the joints appear to be somewhat rounded. The captious critics might say that he is over-long of his back. Undoubtedly his best points lie in front of the saddle. There is a rhythmical quality about the set of his neck, shoulder, and powerful forearm which is carried down through the flat knees to a hard, clean underpin-

1954 Epsom Derby winner Never Say Die, the first Kentucky-bred winner of the historic race. (Courtesy of Bennett Bell Williams)

ning."[2] The most notable feature on the handsome colt was still the prominent white blaze that ran the length of his head—from above his eyes to the tip of his nose—making him easy to pick out of a crowd.

The chestnut-colored colt's racing career began in a less-than-auspicious fashion with a sixth-place effort in a five-furlong race for nonwinners at Newmarket called the May Maiden Stakes. The result in his first outing gave no indication of the success the colt would later achieve, but he had at least been competitive and had shown Lawson enough to warrant a try in the New Stakes at Royal Ascot, the prestigious early-summer meeting faithfully patronized by British high society. That race, now known as the Norfolk Stakes, dated back to 1843 and was a top sprint for two-year-olds run at five furlongs. For his second start,

Never Say Die was given a new rider, top Australian jockey Scobie Breasley. Despite the change, the results were no different: Never Say Die again finished sixth.

Never Say Die then returned to the Ascot turf and won the six-furlong Rosslyn Stakes for his third jockey, Manny Mercer, who was fresh off a victory in that year's One Thousand Guineas and had won the inaugural running of the Washington D.C. International Stakes the previous year.[3] In the Rosslyn Stakes, Never Say Die was well back of the field after two furlongs and had to be asked by his jockey to keep up in the early going. Mercer made an effective late move to win by two lengths against overmatched opponents, but the performance suggested that Never Say Die's late-running style might be better suited for longer races. There was plenty about his pedigree to lend credence to that belief. In addition to his speedy and precocious ancestors the Flying Filly and The Tetrarch, there were a number of American and European classic winners in his pedigree, including Man o' War, War Admiral, Nearco, Blenheim, and Sir Gallahad. But Never Say Die would have to wait until the following year to try added distance. In the meantime, he would continue to be tested in top two-year-old sprinting company.

Next up was the Richmond Stakes at Goodwood in West Sussex, where Scobie Breasley reunited with Never Say Die to finish a good third in the six-furlong race—one that had been won in years past by top horses such as the Aga Khan's Mahmoud and the Young Alec Taylor trainee Bayardo. After a disappointing fifth-place finish in the seven-furlong Solario Stakes at Sandown, Never Say Die and Breasley finished the year on a relative high note with a third-place finish in the prestigious Dewhurst Stakes back at Newmarket.[4] Though Never Say Die had failed to reach the top of his class as a two-year-old, it had been a successful juvenile campaign for a horse whose pedigree indicated he could improve with longer races the next year.

In his year-end review, leading racing commentator Phil Bull

Sculpture of Never Say Die. *Thoroughbred Horse (Never Say Die)* (circa 1955), by John Benson How (American, born 1884); bronze, 8½ inches. (Image 1955.573, © Sterling and Francine Clark Art Institute, Williamstown, Massachusetts; photo by Michael Agee)

observed, "Never Say Die, who is a very good looker, is clearly at least a stone [fourteen pounds] below the top of the tree, and unless he shows abnormal improvement would not therefore merit consideration for any of the Classic races. However, he is certain to make a goodish three-year-old."[5] Joe Lawson had every intention of doing all he could to encourage Never Say Die to make "abnormal improvement." The aging trainer's sights were set squarely on the race that had eluded him during his long and illustrious career: the Epsom Derby, which would be run the following June. Due to Never Say Die's running style, a pedigree that included multiple Triple Crown winners, and a dam that had won at 1¼ miles, there was plenty of reason for hope.

As Lawson looked forward to the colt's three-year-old season, he suspected that a jockey change might help. He decided to give young Lester Piggott a chance to pilot the colt in what Lawson hoped would be a run toward the English classics. If anyone was destined to become a jockey, it was Lester Keith Piggott. He was born in 1935 on Guy Fawkes Day (an English holiday commemorating the failure of the seventeenth-century Gunpowder Plot to assassinate the king and overthrow the government) in the local hospital at Wantage in Oxfordshire, a town whose claim to fame was being the birthplace of King Alfred the Great. The branches of Piggott's family tree were dotted with jockeys and horsemen and -women dating back to the 1700s. His grandfather Ernie Piggott had won the Grand National, England's most prestigious steeplechase, three times as a jockey. Lester's grandmother came from a long line of riders that included her two Derby-winning brothers. Lester's father, Keith, was a successful jockey, winning 500 races over a thirty-year career before becoming a champion trainer of jumpers. Lester's mother, Iris, was also descended from a long line of top-notch jockeys and trainers and was an accomplished rider in her own right. Iris twice won the Newmarket Town Plate, a 4½-mile amateur race that dated back to the reign of Charles II and, at the time, was the only race in England open to women riders.[6]

Lester was named for his mother's brother, a prodigiously talented rider named Frederick Lester Rickaby Jr., who won the One Thousand Guineas four times in five years before losing his life at age twenty-four on a French battlefield at the end of World War I. Given his parents' love of horse racing and the long family tradition of riding, it is not surprising that Keith and Iris's only child, Lester, was in the saddle by the age of two. His mother taught him the basics of horsemanship on his first pony, named Brandy. Brandy stood only thirteen hands (fifty-two inches) tall, but she was spirited and had a propensity to "bolt," taking her rider on high-speed gallops with little notice. So from a very young age, Lester learned how to handle horses running at breakneck speeds. At first his father would allow Lester to climb aboard some of the horses he trained only after they had finished their morning gallops, but by age ten, Lester was a regular morning exercise rider. Given his background and the environment in which he was raised, it is not surprising that Piggott would later admit, "I never seriously considered any walk of life other than racing."[7]

A severe congenital hearing impairment contributed to Lester's lack of interest in school, but it probably also contributed to his relationship with horses; while riding, he was able to block out distractions and focus on the task at hand much more completely than other riders could. Under his father's tutelage, Lester developed his skill in the saddle during morning training sessions, and by age twelve he was ready to try his hand at race riding. While out of school on Easter holiday in April 1948, Lester got his first professional mount in an apprentice-only race at Salisbury on a three-year-old filly named The Chase, which Lester had been exercising for his father. Lester and The Chase finished far back, but the young rider was thrilled by the experience, and as soon as he dismounted, he asked his father when he could do it again. The young jockey's first ride was good enough to convince his father to give him a few more opportunities that summer, and in August, Lester and The Chase were reunited for a race at Haydock that was open to journeyman jockeys.

The top competition that day appeared to be a horse named Prompt Corner, which, until three months prior, had been trained by Keith Piggott. The new trainer, Ginger Dennistoun, was late arriving to the racecourse, and when he finally showed up, Ginger told Prompt Corner's jockey, Davy Jones, not to bother trying to win because he hadn't had an opportunity to place a bet on the horse (and he wanted the chance to make an even bigger score next time, coming off a loss).[8] On the racetrack, as the field thundered toward the finish line, Lester heard Jones, positioned just behind him, yelling at him to hurry up as Jones pulled on the reins to slow his own mount. Lester followed Jones's instructions and crossed the finish line first, with Prompt Corner just behind him.

It was an unusual way to win his first race, but Lester gave no indication that anything was amiss. He quickly attracted attention from the racing press as a wunderkind, but his parents made certain that Lester remained grounded, with his ego firmly in check, and that his daily routine remained unaffected by his budding celebrity. Lester started the following racing season with high hopes, but it would take him until August to reach the winner's circle again, although he did finish the season strongly, ending the year with six victories.

In 1950, while still splitting time between the racetrack and school, Lester rode 52 winners in 404 starts. He was starting to live up to his premature celebrity, and his star seemed to be on the rise, but the following year would be only a mixed bag for Lester. He was ecstatic to make his first Derby start on a promising son of Nasrullah named Zucchero.[9] But that excitement was quickly dashed at the Derby starting line when his mount displayed some of his father's quirky temperament and refused to budge when the starter gave the signal. Once he was reluctantly convinced to begin running, Zucchero made a decent showing, but he had left himself too much ground to recover. A broken leg ended Piggott's racing year early in 1951, and the pressures that accompanied his early success and attention began to mount, as did his weight as he grew into his five-foot seven-inch frame.

In 1953 Lester's win total fell from seventy-nine the previous year to forty-one. It appeared that he would follow the course of many promising young jockeys who grew too big to make the weight required of flat-race jockeys and turn to jump racing, where jockeys were allowed to carry considerably more weight than their flat-racing counterparts. Lester participated in the English jumping season in the winter of 1953–1954, but he also redoubled his efforts to maintain his weight. He was committed to becoming a top rider on the flat, and by the time flat season arrived in the spring of 1954, he was ready to live up to the lofty expectations he had established for himself as a young rider.

Trainer Joe Lawson believed that Piggott was ready to rebound in 1954, and, with Sterling Clark's encouragement, he enlisted the eighteen-year-old to ride Never Say Die in the Union Jack Stakes in Liverpool in late March, the colt's first race in what they hoped would be a momentous year. At that time, the Liverpool meeting was the second of the English season, following a three-day meet at Lincoln. Lester had never been on Never Say Die before, but he later recalled that he connected with the colt immediately, detecting no signs that Never Say Die had inherited the same bullheadedness of his sire that Zucchero and others had. Piggott later remembered the colt as being "a tough, easygoing type . . . simplicity itself to ride."[10]

In his first race as a three-year-old, and the first with his new jockey, Never Say Die was not quite at full fitness; Lawson wanted to bring him along slowly, with the Derby in June being the ultimate goal. Though they lost by a length to Lester's cousin Bill Rickaby riding a colt named Tudor Honey, it was a promising start to the year. Tudor Honey had won an important stakes race the prior year as a two-year-old, and under the circumstances, a respectable second was encouraging.

On the heels of that debut, bettors made Never Say Die the favorite in his next race, the Free Handicap at Newmarket, run at seven furlongs on the Rowley Mile, an undulating straight course whose origins can be traced to the era of King Charles II. Though his connections knew that Never Say Die's optimal distance was farther than seven furlongs, they were troubled by his dismal performance; he started slowly and was never a factor in the race, finishing near the back of the pack with Lester aboard. Doubts about their prospects for making the Derby field began to creep into the minds of jockey and trainer.

Lawson decided to run the colt again two weeks later, this time in the 1¼-mile Newmarket Stakes, in an attempt to prove, at least to himself, that greater distance was all the colt required. But Never Say Die would be without his regular rider, because Piggott chose to ride at Bath (where he had two winners at the two-day meet) rather than remain at Newmarket. Manny Mercer, who rode in Lester's place, encountered a series of troubles early in the race but managed to take the lead coming out of "the Dip," a distinctive valley in the Rowley Mile course one furlong from the finish line. Never Say Die then tired in the final uphill eighth of a mile to finish third, beaten by just a half-length and a head by the winner, Elopement.[11] There was reason for optimism in the Never Say Die camp, however, as the added distance was clearly to the colt's liking. But a postrace miscommunication almost cost Never Say Die a chance at the Derby.

When discussing the race with Lawson and Piggott, Clark's English racing manager, Gerald McElligott, misunderstood the explanation for the horse's loss. Never Say Die had a tendency to lug to the left, especially as he tired at the end of his races, but McElligott reported to Clark via transatlantic cable that the horse had lugged to the *right*. That tendency would be a handicap at the Derby because of the counterclockwise layout of the racecourse at Epsom—a "left-handed" course in racing parlance. Fortunately, Lawson discovered the miscommunication and assured McElligott that Never Say Die should be entered, hoping that his left-leaning tendencies would work to his advantage in the big race. McElligott relayed the recommendation to Clark, adding, "He's a good colt and improving. You should run him." Clark responded, "If you want to run him, go right ahead and do it."[12]

With that decision made, Lawson's only problem was deciding who should ride Never Say Die in the Derby. Given his current form, the colt was not considered a favorite in the big race, a fact reflected by his 200–1 odds just weeks before the Derby.

Piggott's decision to abandon Never Say Die in his final prep race had knocked him from top consideration, but leading jockeys were not lining up for the job. Lawson's first three choices were already booked to ride other horses and, given Never Say Die's outside chances, were not inclined to make a switch. So Lawson offered Piggott the opportunity to reunite with Never Say Die, and the rider gladly accepted. After he was assured of the Derby mount, Piggott had a suggestion for the colt's trainer. In an attempt to correct his horse's left-leaning tendencies, Lawson had used a shadow roll (a fluffy piece of sheepskin attached to the noseband to focus the horse's attention directly in front of him—more commonly used in America than in Europe) and had added some pieces to the horse's bit. Piggott suggested that Lawson remove the corrective devices and allow the horse his natural tendencies, which could prove beneficial on the counterclockwise Epsom course.[13]

The Epsom Derby provides one of the most stringent tests of a horse's mettle in all of Thoroughbred racing. It requires the stamina to endure the 1½-mile course with an uphill finish, the tactical speed to maneuver around a large field without losing momentum, and the temperament to maintain composure in the presence of hundreds of thousands of race fans. The course is arranged in an imperfect horseshoe shape, with the start and finish on opposite endpoints of the U. The first six furlongs are run uphill with a rise of almost 150 feet, the first quarter mile of which includes a slight right-hand bend. At the top of the hill, the course rounds the first of two left-handed turns and continues downhill at varying degrees of steepness. Halfway down the hill, as the horses are gaining momentum, the course again turns sharply to the left at what is known as Tattenham Corner. The finish is a nearly half-mile straightaway that is slightly downhill until the final 100 yards, which provides a grueling uphill finish.

With the aid of hindsight, it is easy to see that Never Say Die possessed the attributes necessary to win a race like the Derby.

He had the rare combination of stamina and tactical speed, as well as the composed disposition to handle the unfettered hubbub that engulfs the Downs on Derby Day. And although he had reformed most of the bad habits displayed as a juvenile delinquent in the bluegrass paddocks where he was raised, Never Say Die still possessed some of the competitive spirit that had caused John A. Bell III to call him "the roughest I ever saw."[14] But those qualifications were not readily apparent to most race fans, and he was still available to the betting public at generous odds as the race drew near.

In the weeks leading up to the Derby, Never Say Die had been thriving in his morning gallops, and, to those paying close attention, he seemed to be coming into himself. The *Daily Telegraph* reported, "Never Say Die may have been a trifle unlucky when third to Elopement at Newmarket. He has given every satisfaction in his work since and should run a good race."[15] Despite some reason for optimism regarding the colt's chances, owner Sterling Clark stayed in New York, choosing not to postpone some tests he was scheduled to undergo at a local hospital. But Clark was often reluctant to attend the races even when he didn't have a good excuse, claiming that race-day crowds "made him nervous."[16]

Never Say Die joined twenty-one rivals on the chilly and damp June afternoon at the Derby starting line. Top contenders included Elopement, to whom Never Say Die had lost his last prep race; Darius, winner of the Two Thousand Guineas; Rowston Manor, winner of the Derby Trial at Lingfield; Ferriol, an invader from France who had finished behind Darius in the Guineas; and the queen's colt, Landau, who had been well beaten by Darius in the Guineas but returned in the Derby Trial to finish a good second to Rowston Manor. Never Say Die was listed by bookmakers as a 33–1 long shot, as was Arabian Night, who had finished behind Never Say Die in his last outing. In the car ride to Epsom with his father that morning, Lester Piggott decided that although Darius's ability to last the entire 1½ miles was questionable, he would likely be among the early leaders in the race; therefore, a good tactic would be to follow behind Darius as far as he lasted.

At the starter's order, Never Say Die, wearing saddlecloth number 5, was away cleanly and fell in just behind the first group of front-runners. Lester sat patiently as the field rounded the first turn, "laying up handy in the early stages, never getting detached from the leading group," he would later recall.[17] The pair held fifth position at the top of the hill and maintained that spot as they headed into Tattenham Corner. Rounding the final turn, Never Say Die was positioned just behind Rowston Manor, Landau, Darius, and Blue Sail, who was ridden by top American jockey Johnny Longden and was quickly losing ground. As Darius took the lead early in the final stretch, Lester moved his horse to the outside and began to pass tiring rivals. Piggott explained that, after accelerating with an eighth of a mile to the finish line, Never Say Die "gave me a winning feeling the rest of the way."[18] Arabian Night made a late run to catch Darius for second, but Piggott and Never Say Die were safely in front at that point and galloped on to a relatively easy two-length victory, finishing in a time of 2:35⁴/₅, two seconds off the record set by the Aga Khan's Mahmoud in 1936. Because Clark was not present to lead his horse to the winner's enclosure, as tradition dictated, that task fell to Never Say Die's groom, Alfie Vaus.

Among the happiest people at Epsom that day were the bookmakers, who had taken plenty of money on a large group of horses vying for the status of lukewarm favorite. Few serious gamblers had bet on the winner, however. One older bookie declared, "In my fifty years in business, I cannot recall a worse Derby result for backers, and that is another way of saying it's my best Derby. A few bets were placed on the winner by those attracted by the name, but the big backers hardly gave him a second thought." One of the biggest bookmakers of the era, Alfred

Cope (no doubt happy with the result himself), acknowledged that Never Say Die had drawn support from a number of small bettors (like Mona Best), the kind who might place a bet only once a year. "After all," the bookmaker queried, "how could [they] miss with a horse called Never Say Die?"[19]

Clark would make certain he was present to see his beloved horse win the final leg of the English Triple Crown later that summer, the St. Leger Stakes at Doncaster in South Yorkshire. But Lester Piggott would not be there. Two weeks after his Derby triumph, Never Say Die was entered in the King Edward VII Stakes at Royal Ascot, named for the racing-enthusiast monarch who had helped the Aga Khan gain entry into top English horse circles more than half a century earlier. After again being positioned just behind the front-runners in the early going, Never Say Die was stuck in fourth place behind a wall of horses but full of run as the field made its way into the final straightaway. Piggott spotted a gap between two of the leaders and urged his horse toward it. But the hole closed before he could get through, causing a series of jostling bumps. The ill-timed move cost Never Say Die his momentum, which he failed to recover in time to improve his position, finishing fourth. The local stewards held Piggott responsible for the incident and brought him before the stewards of the Jockey Club, who summarily revoked Piggott's license for the remainder of the season, a decision based in part on what was becoming a reputation for aggressive riding on Piggott's part.

To Never Say Die's critics, the bumping incident and the result of the race were evidence that the colt's Derby victory had been a fluke. Others pointed to the fact that Never Say Die had been denied a chance to perform at his best by rider error; they believed the colt would be primed and ready for his next outing. His next race—and, as it turned out, his final one—would be the St. Leger Stakes. It would cement Never Say Die's status as one of the top runners of his era. Run on a left-handed course over a distance of more than 1¾ miles, the St. Leger is the oldest and longest of the English classics and a true test of a horse's stamina.

Filling in for Piggott, jockey Charlie Smirke held Never Say Die at the back of the sixteen-horse field at the start, biding his time until he began to improve his position with a mile to go. As the field moved on to the final straight, Never Say Die was in ninth place, still twelve lengths behind the leader. A quarter mile from the finish, Smirke gave his horse the call to quicken, and Never Say Die demolished the field, winning by a whopping dozen lengths. An overjoyed Clark greeted the colt after the race with a big kiss, a hug, and a mouthful of candy as he was being unsaddled. As he fought through tears of joy before some 200,000 fans, Clark declared, "I'm too old to celebrate, but I'm just about the happiest man in the world today."[20]

By annihilating the St. Leger field, Never Say Die left no doubt about his ability or his class. He also flattered his sire Nasrullah, confirming that the stallion, which had demonstrated precocity and speed on the racetrack, was capable of siring runners that could carry that speed over any distance. The victory fully justified the high price the American syndicate had paid for Nasrullah, for it now possessed a sire whose offspring were winning top races on both sides of the Atlantic. Those who believed in the unquestionable superiority of English bloodstock could not easily ignore two dominant victories in two English classics by an American horse for an American owner. The fact that Never Say Die's sire had once stood in England, had been lost to a group of Americans, and appeared to have his best days ahead of him only made things more frustrating for English owners, breeders, and racing fans.

Clark and Lawson had planned to finish Never Say Die's season at the Jockey Club Stakes at Newmarket, but when Clark realized that a victory in that race would move him past Queen Elizabeth into first place in the owners' rankings for the year, he decided to retire his horse instead. Clark felt he was undeserving of the title, as his earnings were overwhelmingly the product of his one top horse, and he did not want to be the one to deny Her Majesty such an honor.

Never Say Die was invited to compete in the Washington D.C. International Stakes at Laurel Park in Maryland, but Clark declined the honor, presumably unwilling to end his boycott of American racing even for such a prestigious event.[21] First run in 1952, the International drew top horses from all over the world and was an important precursor to modern international racing events such as the Breeders' Cup and the Dubai World Cup. It was discontinued after the 1994 running, by which time it had been overshadowed by other international races. Inaugurated at a time when grass racing was still something of a novelty in the United States, the International Stakes both acknowledged the beginning of the globalization of the sport of Thoroughbred racing and helped further it.

Upon retirement, Never Say Die was in high demand as a stallion. Clark had plenty of options when deciding where to send him for stud duty, but he chose to keep Never Say Die in England. The horse spent his first four seasons at Lord Derby's Woodland Stud, where he commanded a stud fee of $1,470, but upon the expiration of his initial contract with Lord Derby, Clark donated Never Say Die, valued at $700,000, to the National Stud in Newmarket for stallion duty, beginning with the 1959 breeding season.[22] Clark, who had not raced in the United States since the end of World War II, cited "my great love for the British nation" as his reason for making the gift.[23] Had he been so inclined, Clark could have brought Never Say Die back to the United States to stand at the breeding farm of his choosing, and he could have demanded top dollar for the colt's services. But pecuniary interests did not motivate Clark, especially at that late stage of his life. Though Clark had to pay a sizable gift tax as a result of his donation, he did not complain.

The winds of change that had brought top European stallions like Nasrullah to the United States would not be shifted by Clark's decision to keep Never Say Die in Britain, however. Following World War II, American racing was more popular than ever and enjoyed a virtual monopoly on legal gambling in America. There was far more money available to owners and breeders in America than in England, and that trend would continue. Clark was anything but an American jingoist when it came to international racing. His own quarrels with American racing authorities were well documented, and he was far more comfortable racing in England and Europe; his decision to stand Never Say Die in England upon his retirement reflected that preference. The irony, therefore, is that despite his disinclination to run his horses in the United States, Sterling Clark contributed significantly to the ascendancy of American Thoroughbreds with his victories in two English classics.

Never Say Die's wins in the 1954 Derby and St. Leger Stakes were a harbinger of a shift in the balance of power in the world of Thoroughbred breeding—a shift from Great Britain to the United States. Evidence of the change had been perceptible as early as the controversial syndication deals that brought stallions such as Blenheim and Sir Gallahad to the United States, and the importation of Nasrullah had continued the trend. The shift would become fully apparent in the decades to come as the offspring of top American sires began to compete more regularly and more successfully in Europe's top races, sending international horsemen to America in droves in search of the world's best bloodstock.

Chapter 9

An American Invasion at Epsom

Never Say Die's progeny had only mixed success as runners overall, but he was the leading sire in Great Britain in 1962. That year, his son Larkspur won the Epsom Derby for Irish trainer Vincent O'Brien (the first of six Derby wins in his legendary career) and American owner Raymond R. Guest.[1] With Larkspur's victory, Never Say Die became the first Epsom Derby winner to sire an Epsom Derby winner since Blenheim II's son Mahmoud won the 1936 Derby for the Aga Khan. The results of the 1962 Derby made headlines around the world, and not only because it was the first Derby victory for an American owner since Never Say Die's win eight years earlier. Six horses finished the race riderless, and one had to be destroyed after breaking its leg in an ugly pileup at Tattenham Corner. Race fans jumped fences to attend to the fallen jockeys until the ambulances arrived. Winning rider Neville Sellwood described his ride more in terms of survival than of triumph. "The horses all fell right in front of me," he recalled. "I had a wonderful escape. Somehow we managed to get through that heap of kicking horses. Once we got into the straight, I knew we would win."[2]

That same day, just a few miles away from the mess at Ep-

The Beatles, whose humble beginnings included Mona Best's Liverpool coffee club, had achieved global fame by the mid-1960s. (Library of Congress)

som, John Lennon, Paul McCartney, George Harrison, and Pete Best, having just returned from their final long-term engagement in Hamburg, Germany, made their first trip to Abbey Road studios in London to record some demo tracks for what would eventually become the Beatles' debut album, *Please Please Me*. Less than three months later, Best was sacked as the band's drummer and replaced by Ringo Starr. Following the modest success of their first single, "Love Me Do," in the fall of 1962, the Beatles built a huge following in Britain. By 1964, "Beatlemania" had spread worldwide. That year, six Beatles singles reached the top of the American pop charts. The next year they had five more number-one hits.[3] Even after the group stopped touring in 1966, it continued to produce chart-topping records, including the groundbreaking LPs *Revolver* and *Sgt. Pepper's Lonely Hearts Club Band*. Meanwhile, Pete Best had survived a suicide attempt at the height of Beatlemania and would be out of the music busi-

Pete Best, circa 2006. Unceremoniously ousted from the group prior to the onset of Beatlemania, Best temporarily abandoned music in the late 1960s but returned to professional drumming two decades later.

ness by year's end. The lads from Liverpool were revolutionizing rock and roll, whose roots were so deeply American, just as Americans were starting to achieve similar sustained success in England, the birthplace of Thoroughbred racing, at the Epsom Derby.

In the spring of 1968 the Beatles returned from their well-publicized spiritual retreat to India. As the group was beginning work on a new album that would eventually be popularly known as the *White Album*, Lester Piggott won his fourth English Derby with an "electrifying surge in the final yards" on Sir Ivor, who was owned and trained by the same combination that had captured the Derby six years earlier with Never Say Die's son Larkspur.[4]

At the start of the race, Piggott urged Sir Ivor quickly out of the starting gate (first introduced to the Derby the year before) and secured a position in the middle of the pack in the early going. The front-runners began to fade as the field headed downhill toward Tattenham Corner. Piggott improved his position but still trailed long-distance specialist Connaught by a good margin. With two furlongs to go, Piggott and Sir Ivor were still four lengths behind the leader. It was time to move, so Piggott pulled his horse to the outside to give him room for a final burst of speed. For a moment, the horse did not respond; then a light seemed to go on in the horse's head, and he understood what was being asked of him. Sir Ivor flew past Connaught with 100 yards to the finish and cruised to victory.

In the *Daily Mirror* Bob Butchers called Piggott's ride "one of the greatest performances of race riding that Lester Piggott, or any other jockey for that matter, has ever executed. The sheer cheek of the champion had to be seen to be believed." The *Daily Telegraph* praised Lester's ride as "a performance which for sheer style and flawless elegance has surely never been bettered at Epsom Downs."[5]

Those who had witnessed the remarkable race were equally effervescent in their praise of Sir Ivor, who became the first odds-on winner of the Derby since Gainsborough in 1918.[6] John Lawrence wrote in the *Daily Telegraph*, "I honestly believe that Mr. Raymond Guest's Sir Ivor must be about as close as man has ever come to success in his long search for the ideal Thoroughbred." He continued, "[Sir Ivor is] a beautiful well-oiled machine who handles like a London taxi and accelerates like an Aston Martin. He is, in a word, perfection, and has in Vincent O'Brien and Lester Piggott the sort of accomplices that such perfection deserves."[7] The man with the best view of all was nineteen-year-old jockey Sandy Barclay, who thought he had the Derby won on Connaught with only yards to go. "Sir Ivor went past me as though he had just jumped in," Barclay recalled. "[He] is the most brilliant horse I have ever seen."[8] Even Piggott would later call the talented bay "the best horse I ever rode," quite a weighty statement from a man who had won nine Epsom Derbies.[9]

Never Say Die and Robert Sterling Clark had reminded the racing world that it was possible for an American horse to win England's top horse race, and with the transatlantic transportation of horses by air becoming commonplace, increasing numbers of wealthy American sportsmen were making the Derby a top priority for their American runners. Before Never Say Die won the English Derby, the only other American-bred horse to win the race (which was first contested in 1780) had been Iroquois in 1881. But Sir Ivor's 1968 win began a five-year stretch in which American horses and owners won four Epsom Derbies, announcing a shift in the global balance of power in the racing industry and signaling the beginning of a boom time for American bloodstock markets. All four of those Derby winners were descendants of European runners owned by the Aga Khan and sold to American interests. Though this remarkable period of American success at Epsom would be relatively short-lived, its reverberations would be felt for decades.

Bred by Alice Headley at her Mill Ridge Farm in Lexington, Kentucky, and sold as a yearling just up the road at Keeneland, Sir Ivor was owned by Raymond Guest, an American politician, businessman, and diplomat.[10] Guest's great-grandfather was the 7th Duke of Marlborough, and his grandfather was Henry Phipps Jr., Andrew Carnegie's partner in Carnegie Steel. Like Robert Sterling Clark, Guest was not in attendance to see his colt take the Derby, so it was his wife, Caroline, who led Sir Ivor into the winner's enclosure. Guest, the U.S. ambassador to Ireland, was in County Wexford for the dedication of a park named after John F. Kennedy, but he was able to watch the race on television. Guest had had the foresight and confidence to make an early bet on Sir Ivor to win the Derby—at odds of 100–1—the year before, which netted him a return of $148,800 (in addition to the $140,00 first prize as winning owner). Though he had been a relative unknown when Guest made his early bet, Sir Ivor was a 4–5 post-time favorite. His victory cost bookmakers millions.

One bookie called the race "a tale of woe for us. It couldn't have been any worse."[11]

After the Derby, Sir Ivor failed to win any of his next four races, though he was never out of the money. He ended his career on a winning note, however, taking the Washington D.C. International Stakes at Laurel Park in Maryland, becoming the first Epsom Derby winner to compete in the United States since Papyrus in 1923.[12] Inside the race's final furlong, Lester Piggott sent Sir Ivor through a small gap between Carmarthen and Paul Mellon's champion gelding Fort Marcy, holding on at the wire for a three-quarter-length victory.

In 1970 Piggott again captured the Derby Stakes for a Vincent O'Brien trainee, this time aboard Nijinsky for American owner Charles Engelhard. Engelhard had made a fortune in precious metal mines and was rumored to have been an inspiration for Ian Fleming's character Auric Goldfinger in his James Bond series. The winning owner was beside himself after the race. "This is wonderful," he exclaimed. "Every time I've watched my horses run here they seemed to lose. But this certainly makes up for it. My glasses misted up at the finish and I could hardly see a thing."[13] The winning time was the second fastest in the history of the race. Trainer O'Brien, slightly more subdued than the owner, summed up the dominant performance: "We were always cantering. A grand performance."[14] Raymond Guest's brother, Winston, owned the runner-up, an American-bred colt named Gyr. The one-two finish for American owners was a Derby first.[15]

The winning owner, trainer, and jockey were invited to the Royal Box to be congratulated by the queen. It was the first such invitation for Piggott. That night, the team celebrated at a popular London nightspot called Annabel's. Bearing a resemblance to American comedian W. C. Fields, and not in particularly good health, Engelhard kept a case of his beverage of choice, Coca-Cola, next to his chair at the party. He did his best to finish it but fell asleep before dessert was served.

Nijinsky, purchased from Canadian breeder E. P. Taylor by American mining tycoon Charles W. Engelhard Jr. for $84,000, won the 1970 English Triple Crown, becoming the first horse to accomplish that feat since the Aga Khan's Bahram in 1935. (Courtesy of University of Kentucky Archives)

Engelhard had purchased Nijinsky as a yearling at auction from the horse's breeder, Canadian brewing magnate E. P. Taylor, for a Canadian-record $84,000.[16] Nijinsky possessed a regal Canadian pedigree, as both his sire and dam were winners of the Queen's Plate, Canada's oldest and most prestigious Thoroughbred race. Nijinsky was named after the late Russian ballet dancer, who had predicted he would be reincarnated as a horse. The dancer's widow, Romola Nijinsky, had a standing bet with a bookmaker on each of the horse's races, which returned a very tidy profit. Romola had written a letter to Lester Piggott following the first leg of the Triple Crown and told him, "I was tremendously impressed with your magnificent winning of the Two Thousand Guineas race this afternoon on the beautiful horse, Nijinsky, and I send you my congratulations. I ask of you now only one thing—please win the Derby for us!"[17] The widow was in attendance for Nijinsky's Derby score as the guest of Engelhard.[18]

On the heels of his Epsom Derby triumph, Nijinsky won the Irish Derby, becoming just the second English-Irish Derby winner in modern history. Liam Ward, contract rider for Vincent O'Brien in Ireland (but not elsewhere), was reduced to cliché in describing the race: "It was so easy, even my grandmother could have won on this great horse."[19] After a win over older horses in the King George VI and Queen Elizabeth Stakes to increase his lifetime unbeaten string to ten straight, Nijinsky took the St. Leger Stakes at Doncaster to become the first Triple Crown champion in England since the Aga Khan's Bahram in 1935. Observers had run out of superlatives for this superhorse, the fourth St. Leger winner for owner Charles Engelhard. Lester Piggott, who had been reunited with the horse upon Nijinsky's return to England, declared, "I've only got one thing to say. What a horse."[20]

Following his Triple Crown win, many believed Nijinsky could not be beaten. The phrase "wonder horse of all time" was even bandied about. Ward told a reporter, "I'll walk to Tipperary in my birthday suit if Nijinsky ever gets beaten."[21] The historical record does not indicate whether Ward made good on his claim, but Nijinsky finished his career with two disappointing second-place finishes in two weeks.

That Nijinsky was even able to start in the St. Leger represented something of an accomplishment. Weeks before the race he had contracted a bad case of American ringworm, causing him to lose much of his hair and, with it, much of his energy. This disturbed his training schedule to such an extent that his trainer thought they should skip the St. Leger and wait for the Prix de l'Arc de Triomphe in October. But Charles Engelhard was dying, and he wanted to see his horse's name on the exclusive list of Triple Crown winners. Though his victory in the St. Leger appeared to be an easy one, Nijinsky had lost twenty-nine pounds and was a tired horse as he prepared for his next start, in the Arc de Triomphe, just three weeks later.

Nijinsky had become an international celebrity, and Longchamp racecourse in Paris was filled with fans and media hoping to see the undefeated champion add to his legacy in the Arc. A Japanese film crew stuck a microphone under the horse's mouth but could not get a useful quote from him. Amid all the prerace attention, Nijinsky became soaked with sweat, indicating that he had become overly excited. Piggott rode the colt with confidence in the early going on the wide, right-handed Longchamp course. After lagging near the back of the pack for most of the race, Piggott maneuvered Nijinsky to the outside for his patented late burst of speed in the final straight, but Nijinsky lunged left in the stretch (perhaps in response to right-handed whacks from Piggott's whip) and finished a head short of Sassafras at the wire. Piggott explained that "Nijinsky just wasn't himself" that day.[22] But Engelhard felt that Nijinsky's human connections had let the colt down, and he wanted his champion to finish his career on a winning note. Engelhard entered Nijinsky in what he thought would be a certain win in the season-ending Champion Stakes at Newmarket, just thirteen days later. But the long year and the trying experience in France had taken their toll, and Nijinsky again finished second.

Retiring with a stellar record of eleven wins and two seconds in thirteen lifetime starts, Nijinsky was syndicated for a record $5.44 million and would stand as a stallion in Kentucky at Claiborne Farm.[23] In addition to Engelhard, shareholders included top American breeders John Hay Whitney, Paul Mellon, Ogden Phipps, King Ranch's Bob Kleberg, John Galbreath, Buffalo Bills owner Ralph Wilson, and E. P. Taylor, the colt's breeder. An Anglo-Irish group had tried to keep the colt in Britain for stallion duties but had been outbid.

The record syndication would soon prove to be a bargain, as Nijinsky's prodigious stallion career justified the price tag. Among his other accomplishments, Nijinsky sired a half brother to American Triple Crown winner Seattle Slew—later named Seattle Dancer—that would sell as a yearling for a record $13.1

million in 1983. Three years later, Nijinsky would become the first horse to sire the winners of the Kentucky Derby and the English Derby in the same year. He would sire a total of 3 Epsom Derby winners among 155 stakes winners in his legendary stallion career.[24]

The year after Nijinsky won the English Triple Crown, another horse came from "across the pond" to take the Derby, continuing Americans' remarkable run of success at Epsom. This time it was Mill Reef, owned and bred in Virginia by Paul Mellon (son of Andrew W. Mellon), whose Rokeby Farms included land previously occupied by Robert Sterling Clark's neighboring Sundridge Farm, which Mellon had purchased after Clark's death. Mellon had campaigned back-to-back Horse of the Year Award winners in the United States, but even their achievements paled in comparison to those of Mill Reef, a grandson of Nasrullah (his sire, Never Bend, was from Nasrullah's final crop of offspring). In his fourteen career starts, Mill Reef was never worse than second, winning twelve races.

A pattern of American success at Epsom was starting to reveal itself, as Peter Towers-Clark, European racing correspondent for the Kentucky-based *Thoroughbred Record*, noted: "This was the third American-owned and trans-Atlantic-bred winner of the Epsom Derby in the past four years," he reported. "The pendulum is very inclined to swing in racing, but just at this moment it seems that European breeders cannot find the magic formula that appears to be contained in the best of the horses that come over to Europe from the American continent."[25]

After his Derby win, Mill Reef twice defeated older horses that summer in preparation for Europe's premier autumn race, the Prix de l'Arc de Triomphe. Only once in history had a horse captured the Derby Stakes in June and then gone on to win the Arc in October, but Mill Reef had clearly established that he was a special horse. He added to his legacy in the 1971 Arc, easily winning the race by three lengths in record time over a top international field. That field included One For All, owned by a syndicate headed by John A. Bell III, whose equine operation had grown by leaps and bounds since the early days at Hamburg Place. Mill Reef was the first American-owned and American-bred horse to win the Arc, in its fiftieth running.

As a stallion prospect in the United States, Mill Reef would have been extremely valuable. But upon retirement, Mill Reef joined Never Say Die at the National Stud, illustrating that Mellon—like Sterling Clark—was cut from a different cloth. Mirroring the approach of landed English aristocrats of a bygone era, Mellon was more concerned with conducting his equine operation for sport's sake rather than turning a profit. Of course, it was an inherited fortune based on decades-long entrepreneurial efforts that afforded Mellon (as well as Clark) the luxury of disregarding the profitability of his racing endeavors. By contrast, John A. Bell III was very concerned about the profitability of his own expanding equine operation.

Never Say Die's surprise win in the 1954 Derby had helped put Bell on the international Thoroughbred map. Since that time, he had moved his operation from the leased facility at Hamburg Place to a farm on the other side of Lexington; it would eventually encompass almost 800 acres of prime bluegrass land. Bell had purchased the initial tract of what would become the new Jonabell Farm in 1954—the same year Never Say Die won the Derby—with the help of an interest-free loan from Paul Mellon, who was an early client and social acquaintance of Bell's. Before selling the farm to Sheikh Mohammed bin Rashid Al Maktoum of Dubai in 2001, Bell owned, bred, raised, and sold more than 150 stakes winners at Jonabell. He sold four horses for world-record prices and stood a number of champion racehorses as stallions, including Green Forest, Housebuster, Cherokee Run, Holy Bull, and Affirmed.

Paul Mellon was a generous man, giving away hundreds of millions of dollars in his lifetime to various charities, so his de-

John A. Bell III at Jonabell Farm. Never Say Die's success helped Bell establish one of the leading Thoroughbred operations in America. (Courtesy of Bennett Bell Williams)

Jonabell Farm entrance. In 1954, the year of Never Say Die's historic Epsom Derby win, John A. Bell III expanded his Jonabell Farm operation with the purchase of some property on Bowman's Mill Road in Lexington. The purchase was facilitated by an interest-free loan from Paul Mellon. In 2001 the farm was acquired by Sheikh Mohammed bin Rashid Al Maktoum.

cision to loan Bell money at an important juncture in his career was not unprecedented, but it can perhaps be better understood when some of the similarities of their upbringing and personalities are considered. Mellon and Bell shared more than just a love of horses and the sport of Thoroughbred racing. Like Mellon, Bell had been born into a wealthy Pittsburgh family (albeit far less wealthy than the Mellons). And both men found themselves disinclined to follow their fathers into the business world. One can imagine that Mellon saw a bit of himself in the younger Bell and wanted to encourage Bell's decision to pursue his passion professionally. Perhaps Mellon also felt some regret over the fate of Bell's grandfather. Mellon's father had been involved in the series of events that led to Bell's grandfather exiting the Pennsylvania senatorial race at what was the beginning of a dramatic fall from grace that ended in bankruptcy, jail, and death for the elder Bell.

Mellon had studied British literature at Cambridge after graduating from Yale. While studying in England, Mellon developed a lifelong interest in foxhunting and British culture. Though he worked in his father's banks as a young man, he never developed a serious interest in the world of finance. In addition to his charitable donations, horse racing and art collecting became Mellon's lifework. For four decades he served on the board of trustees of the National Gallery of Art in Washington, D.C., which his father had founded, including stints as chairman and president. Andrew W. Mellon had donated his priceless collection of European masterpieces, including works by Rembrandt, Titian, Botticelli, Goya, El Greco, Gainsborough, and Raphael, along with millions of dollars to pay for their upkeep, when he established the National Gallery. Paul himself later founded the Yale Center for British Art with his donation of thousands of British paintings, drawings, prints, and books, along with a building to house and display them and an endowment to maintain them. Upon its opening in 1977, the Yale Center became the largest collection of British art outside of England.

Paul Mellon, oil on canvas, by William Orpen (1878–1931). Heir to his father's immense fortune, Mellon is one of only four owners to win both the Epsom and Kentucky Derbies.

Like Mellon, Robert Sterling Clark left a legacy in the art world that would surpass even that of his racehorses. The year after Clark's Derby triumph with Never Say Die, the Sterling and Francine Clark Art Institute opened to the public on the campus of Williams College in Williamstown, Massachusetts, from which Clark's grandfather had graduated more than a century earlier. Clark had considered Manhattan and Cooperstown as sites for his collection, but he hoped that Williamstown's location near popular summer vacation destinations in the Berkshire Mountains would attract a broader cross section of visitors.

In establishing the institute and building the museum to house it, Clark donated a sizable amount of money as well as his world-class collection of European and American masterpieces by the likes of Degas, Renoir, Van Dyck, Goya, Winslow Homer, and Frederic Remington. Like the many silver trophies won by their horses on European racecourses and returned to the United States, Clark and Mellon had acquired some of Europe's best paintings and established—in America—two of the world's finest collections and museums.

The year after Mellon's Derby victory with Mill Reef, Lester Piggott and Vincent O'Brien teamed up for another Derby victory, just as they had in 1968 and 1970 with Sir Ivor and Nijinsky. In 1972 their Derby-winning horse was the regally bred Roberto, whose family tree included both Nasrullah's sire Nearco and the Flying Filly, Mumtaz Mahal. An American property developer and skyscraper builder named John W. Galbreath owned and bred Roberto. Born in 1897 in Darby, Ohio, Galbreath was the son of a farmer and the grandson of a Methodist preacher. He showed an adeptness for enterprise at a young age, peddling horseradish as a boy and selling photos of Ohio University students to their parents while he was in college. Galbreath served in World War I before returning to finish his degree, and he eventually parlayed a series of small Depression-era sales commissions on foreclosed properties in Columbus, Ohio, into a real estate development empire. In addition to his farms in Kentucky and Ohio, Galbreath owned Major League Baseball's Pittsburgh Pirates, whose star player was Roberto Clemente. Galbreath named the horse Roberto after his beloved right fielder, who would die tragically in a plane crash on December 31, 1972, while performing humanitarian work to aid earthquake-ravaged Nicaragua.[26]

Galbreath chose Lester Piggott to ride Roberto in the Derby after Bill Williamson, the jockey who had ridden him to a second-place finish in the Two Thousand Guineas, was injured in a spill eleven days before the big race. The decision to change riders was controversial, as Williamson believed himself fit to ride. Williamson's wife called the switch "jolly disgraceful."[27] But even critics of the decision could not argue with the results when Piggott and Roberto just barely outlasted long-shot Rhinegold, ridden by Ernie Johnson, in a grueling duel through the final straight that ended with one of the closest finishes in the history of the race. Galbreath acknowledged his controversial choice in his postrace comments but made no apologies. "I thought Piggott was brilliant," he said. "You've got to be 100 per cent fit for this. I have a lot of experience [with] athletes. The baseball team I own, the Pittsburgh Pirates, has just won the World Series. I know something about fitness and I am convinced that no sportsman who has been out of action for about ten days, as Williamson was, can be 100 per cent fit. It was that factor and nothing else that brought about the switch."[28]

In winning the 1972 Derby, Galbreath became the first person to own and breed a winner of both the Kentucky Derby (which he had won in 1963 and 1967 with Chateaugay and Proud Clarion) and the Epsom Derby. He put the English version on a par with any of the various championships he had won in his sporting career. "Anyone who doesn't consider the Epsom Derby one of the greatest sporting events in the world must be out of his mind," Galbreath opined.[29] For Piggott, the Derby win was his record-tying sixth, but more telling for the overall balance of power in the global Thoroughbred industry was the fact that Roberto's victory marked the fourth time in five years that the winning horse had come from North America to capture England's great race for an American owner.

One person who could claim as much responsibility as anyone for the American success at Epsom was trainer Vincent O'Brien. His charges Blue Larkspur, Sir Ivor, Nijinsky, and Roberto had won four Derbies in the decade between 1962 and 1972, during which time the Irish trainer clearly established himself as the top developer of runners in all of Europe. O'Brien had begun his training career with jumpers, winning each of the top three English jumping events—the Grand National, the Cheltenham Gold Cup, and the Champion Hurdle—three times in succession.

His seamless transition to flat racing had made Ballydoyle—the training complex in County Tipperary, Ireland, where O'Brien worked his magic—a household name among racing fans. O'Brien was already being mentioned as one of the greatest Thoroughbred trainers of all time, but many of his best accomplishments were yet to come. Of O'Brien's many admirers in the world of horse racing, none would be more significant than Robert Sangster, whose deep pockets, combined with O'Brien's keen eye, would produce the most successful buying spree in the history of horse racing, forever changing the Thoroughbred industry in the process.

Chapter 10

A Global Sport and Industry

Robert Sangster grew up in suburban Liverpool and was the sole heir to a family fortune that included a quasi-national lottery based on the scores of English soccer matches called Vernons Pools. He was first introduced to horse racing in 1960 when a friend gave him a tip on a horse owned by the friend's grandfather that was entered in a traditional English early-spring fixture, the Lincolnshire Handicap. Sangster lost a 50-pound bet on the horse named Chalk Stream but became hopelessly hooked on the sport in the process. He then bought Chalk Stream for 1,000 pounds as a gift for his wife, beginning an active involvement with racing that would last the rest of his life. Years later, Sangster would purchase Manton, the training yard and estate where Never Say Die's trainer Joe Lawson plied his trade for so many years, making it the center of his juggernaut English racing program. But it was Sangster's relationship with Vincent O'Brien that would make all his subsequent racing success possible and, in the process, forever alter the sport and business of international Thoroughbred racing.

Sangster first met O'Brien at the July 1972 Keeneland yearling sales in Lexington, Kentucky, weeks after Roberto's Derby triumph. The casual but momentous introduction was made by a young Irish horseman named John Magnier. Originally from

County Cork, Magnier came from a long line of Thoroughbred breeders and hoped to return the Irish Thoroughbred breeding industry to the place of prominence it had lost. He lamented the fact that Nijinsky had been syndicated and returned to America for stallion duty and hoped that Ireland would someday be able to afford to keep top stallions. He had a plan to realize that vision, but he needed capital. Sangster had money, and O'Brien's record of getting the best out of top racehorses stood for itself. The three men, who would later be known as the Brethren in racing circles, formed a partnership that became the most formidable the horse industry had ever seen.

In 1973 O'Brien and Sangster bought Coolmore Stud in County Tipperary, Ireland, and established Magnier (who would soon become O'Brien's son-in-law) as manager. The Brethren then planned their strategy to wrest top American bloodlines from the United States via auctions, particularly the July yearling sale at Keeneland. Keeneland's summer sale had been born out of necessity in the face of travel restrictions during World War II, which made it impossible for many Bluegrass State horsemen to travel to Saratoga, New York, the site of Fasig-Tipton's annual summer yearling sale. By the 1970s, the Keeneland July sale had become the world's premier horse sale, and the Brethren were shopping for the world's best yearlings. Their plan centered around Sangster's theory that "the only man who can make money out of buying the best and most expensive yearlings is, in the end, the man who buys them all."[1]

The market for stallion shares and seasons in America was seriously heating up, as evidenced by the recent syndication of Nijinsky and of Nasrullah's grandson, American Triple Crown winner Secretariat, for over $6 million.[2] That market would grow as promising young stallion prospects such as Seattle Slew, Affirmed, and Spectacular Bid emerged later in the decade.[3] Equine superstars on both sides of the Atlantic were keeping horse racing on the front pages of newspapers, helping to spur demand for young horses. The Brethren saw that it would be cheaper to buy stallion prospects before they had demonstrated their ability on the racetrack, assuming the right ones could be identified early. "Baby stallions, Robert, that's what we're after," Magnier told Sangster. O'Brien agreed with the strategy and had particular notions regarding where those baby stallions could be found. "We must buy all the Northern Dancers," O'Brien declared. "We must buy them at all costs. And the same goes for yearlings by Nijinsky. I am telling you. We must have them. I am very certain of that."[4]

Northern Dancer was a small but extremely talented race-horse that had narrowly missed winning the American Triple Crown in 1964. He won the Kentucky Derby in record time and followed that historic performance with a victory in the Preakness Stakes, but he finished third in the Belmont Stakes. That year he also won the Queen's Plate in Canada, as well as the Florida Derby, Flamingo Stakes, and Blue Grass Stakes, on his way to being named Horse of the Year in Canada and champion three-year-old colt in the United States. He shared with Never Say Die some common ancestry: the Aga Khan's Derby-winning son Blenheim; his gray-colored "Flying Filly," Mumtaz Mahal; and Federico Tesio's undefeated phenomenon Nearco appeared prominently in the pedigrees of both champions. Additionally, Northern Dancer was inbred to Gainsborough, the horse that Alec Taylor Jr. had trained to the English Triple Crown.

Northern Dancer began his stud career in his native Canada after retiring from the racetrack in 1964. In his small first crop of offspring, which started racing in 1968, he sired ten stakes winners from twenty-one foals. The following year he was moved to Maryland, where he remained for the rest of his career. At the height of his popularity in the 1980s, Northern Dancer attracted a stud fee that reportedly reached $1 million.[5] His progeny regularly fetched top prices at Kentucky yearling sales, peaking at an unprecedented $10.2 million in 1983.

The Brethren took aim at the American yearling market and started their incursion at the July 1975 yearling sales. Among their purchases that year was a small chestnut son of Northern Dancer with four white stockings. He was out of a daughter of Nijinsky's dam, making him closely related to the English Triple Crown winner himself. The colt's relatively inexpensive price of $200,000 could be attributed to the diminutive size he inherited from his father (and perhaps to his white stockings, which some horsemen believed was an indication of weak bone). "I was definitely concerned about his height," O'Brien later recalled. "I remember going back to his box more than once to see if I could make myself feel any easier about it. But he was certainly small. He did grow in the end. He finished just short of 15.3 hands. But again, this Northern Dancer breed was something new in the racehorse world. They don't have to be big to be good."[6]

The little colt would be called The Minstrel. In 1976 he won all three of his starts as a two-year-old, but that was not enough to convince some skeptics of his prospects for the next year's Derby. For instance, Timeform's *Racehorses of 1976* stated: "Judging from his pedigree, we should say that there is no room for doubt that The Minstrel will stay a mile and a quarter, but that it is by no means certain that he will stay a mile and a half. In which case the 2,000 Guineas would seem the race most likely to provide him with success in a Classic. Granted normal luck in running, The Minstrel will be hard to beat at Newmarket [in the Two Thousand Guineas]."[7]

That year at Epsom, Lester Piggott became the all-time leader in career English Derby wins by a jockey with his seventh. His winning mount that day was Empery—yet another American-bred and American-owned winner of the Derby. Empery upset heavily favored (and undefeated) Wallow, to the delight of the legions of punters who backed Lester's Derby horse every year, regardless of form or pedigree. Empery was owned and bred by Texas oil billionaire Nelson Bunker Hunt, who would later famously tell the U.S. Congress, "People who know how much they're worth aren't usually worth that much."[8] He made the statement during a hearing stemming from allegations that Hunt had attempted to corner the global silver market. Hunt had entered the silver business in 1973, after Libya nationalized his 8-million-acre oil holdings there.[9] Four days after Empery's Derby win, Hunt's colt named Youth would win the French Derby, making Hunt the first American to win both the French and English Derbies.[10] A year earlier Hunt had narrowly missed winning the Epsom Derby when his filly Nobiliary finished second, the best Derby finish by a filly in more than half a century.[11]

Empery was sired by Irish-bred Vaguely Noble, who won the 1968 Arc de Triomphe before being retired for stallion duty at Gainesway Farm in Kentucky with a syndication value of $5 million. Hunt had raced Vaguely Noble in partnership with Los Angeles plastic surgeon Robert A. Franklyn, who helped popularize silicone breast implants and had once immodestly declared, "I know more about beauty than anyone in the world. I have that kind of ego and I believe that about myself. I am the man who showed women that they could compete with Jane Russell. I enlarged the breast line of America when everyone said that it couldn't be done."[12] Empery would be retired following a second-place finish in the 1976 Irish Derby, but Lester Piggott was already looking forward to what he confidently believed would be a championship season for The Minstrel the following year.

To begin his 1977 three-year-old campaign, The Minstrel won the Two Thousand Guineas Trial at Ascot, but the ground was soggy and he struggled over it. In his next race, the small chestnut colt finished third as the heavy favorite in the Two Thousand Guineas, raising serious doubts about his ability to stay longer than a mile. The Brethren needed classic wins to market a horse as a top-level stallion, and they thought that the Irish Two Thousand Guineas would be an easy opportunity for The

Winner of the 1968 Prix de l'Arc de Triomphe, Vaguely Noble was syndicated for a world-record $5 million and brought to Gainesway Farm in Kentucky for stallion duty. (Courtesy of University of Kentucky Archives)

Minstrel. But again he was defeated, leaving his owners with little confidence about his prospects in the Epsom Derby.

But Lester Piggott remained hopeful. "If you run him, I'll ride him. On decent ground, he'll win," Piggott told Robert Sangster in the jockeys' room after the loss.[13] With that vote of confidence, O'Brien and the owners decided to give The Minstrel a shot in the Derby. The bettors had not lost faith in the colt and made him second favorite behind the French colt Blushing Groom, owned by the grandson of Aga Khan III, who had succeeded his grandfather as leader of the Ismailis.

Born Prince Karim Aga Khan in Switzerland in 1936, Aga Khan IV became the forty-ninth imam of the Ismaili Muslims at age twenty, upon his grandfather's death. The third Aga Khan's will, released to the press following a family meeting at his villa outside Geneva, Switzerland, provided the official reason why he had chosen to bypass his son, Aly Khan, in favor of his grandson, then an undergraduate student at Harvard: "In view of the fundamentally altered conditions in the world in very recent years due to the great changes that have taken place, including the discoveries of atomic science, I am convinced that it is in the best interests of the Shia Muslim Ismaili community that I should be succeeded by a young man who has been brought up and developed during recent years and in the midst of the new age, and who brings a new outlook on life to his office."[14]

Despite these nominal justifications for choosing Karim rather than Aly, Aga Khan III had been troubled by his son's lifestyle for years. Although Aly was known for his military service to the Allies during World War II and for his work on behalf of the United Nations after the war, including serving as Pakistan's representative to the international body, he also had a legendary appetite for fast cars, beautiful women, and fast and beautiful horses. He was a champion amateur jockey and a world-class playboy. He had two high-profile marriages and divorces—the second of which was to Hollywood starlet Rita Hayworth—among other high-profile love affairs. "Ah, if Aly would only choose his women as well as he does his horses," the Aga Khan had lamented.[15]

In addition to his title, Karim inherited his grandfather's deep devotion to the improvement of the lives of his followers through economic uplift programs. Like his grandfather, he collected tithes from his followers but also invested millions in projects that created jobs and empowered Ismailis in the developing world. After some initial hesitancy, Aga Khan IV also acquired his grandfather's and father's love of horse racing and breeding. His father, Aly, had died in an automobile crash in Paris less than three years after his own father's death. Aly had spent the last day of his life at Longchamp racecourse. "Don't play my horse today, I don't feel lucky," he told a friend before heading home to dress for a dinner party.[16] As a horseman, Aly Khan may have just been reaching his stride. The year before his death, he won the Arc de Triomphe with his three-year-old colt Saint Crespin, as well as the English One Thousand Guineas and the Oaks with his gray filly Petite Etoile, setting records for purse money won in a year in both Great Britain and France. Though Aly Khan had many successes as an owner and a breeder of world-class race-horses, he never won the Epsom Derby. His son Karim would do so four times, but in 1977, when his colt Blushing Groom (the previous year's champion two-year-old in France) was looming as the favorite, he had yet to win his first.[17]

On Derby Day in 1977, Britain was celebrating Queen Elizabeth's Silver Jubilee, and the Derby crowd of around 250,000 was particularly lively. Trainer Vincent O'Brien stuffed cotton in The Minstrel's ears to dampen the noise of the crowd. The colt behaved like a gentleman before the race and gave a performance to match on the racecourse, which was, as Piggott had hoped, not too soft. With two furlongs to go, only two horses remained in contention for victory—The Minstrel and Hot Grove. They battled neck and neck to the finish line, with The Minstrel prevailing by a nose. Blushing Groom, better suited for shorter distances, took third. It seemed to observers that Piggott had simply willed his horse to win, and many called his performance the finest of his distinguished career. "Lester Piggott crowned a glorious career with a Jubilee gem in yesterday's Derby," the *Daily Mail* reported. "He has ridden a host of great races but this win was the finest of them all. This was Piggott the Supreme at his superb best, riding at a peak seldom, if ever, reached by any other jockey."[18]

The Minstrel's victory gave Vincent O'Brien his fifth Epsom Derby victory and Lester Piggott his eighth. Plans for the Aga Khan's victory party at Annabel's were quickly changed, and the decorations were switched from the young imam's green and red colors to the blue and green of Robert Sangster. The Aga Khan graciously attended the party as Sangster's guest. Perhaps the sweetest part of The Minstrel's win for the Brethren was that it guaranteed the colt's marketability as a stallion. The Minstrel finished the season, and his career, with victories in the Irish Derby and the King George VI Stakes, adding to his legacy and increasing his value in a booming market. His owners had hoped to keep him in Ireland for stallion duties at their Coolmore Stud, but the money available in America was too great to pass up. They agreed to stand him at the farm of E. P. Taylor, breeder of Northern Dancer, in Maryland. They valued The Minstrel at $9 million for syndication purposes but retained a significant ownership percentage. Before long, the Coolmore team would be able to keep their top racehorses to stand as stallions at their own stud farms.

As the parties negotiated the specifics of The Minstrel's syndication deal, the colt was being trained for a late-season appearance at the Prix de l'Arc de Triomphe in Paris.[19] But an outbreak of equine contagious metritis (inflammation of the uterus) in England led to an American ban on imported horses from affected areas and forced the owners to make a quick decision. They made up their minds to retire the horse and arranged a transatlantic flight for him just before the import ban took effect. Their fast thinking ensured that The Minstrel would be able to stand his first season at stud in the United States the following year, but it ended his racing career prematurely.

The Minstrel was just one of a handful of top-class runners to emerge from the Brethren's initial yearling purchases in 1975 and 1976. In what might be the most successful buying spree in the history of racing, the group landed two classic winners, a two-year-old champion, and a handful of other stakes winners— all in addition to their Derby-winning colt. It appeared that these men from Coolmore Stud had found a formula for success in the commercial bloodstock world: buy all the top stallion prospects as yearlings. Unbeknownst to the Brethren, however, a rival for supremacy in the racing world was waiting in the wings and would irrevocably alter the landscape of the sport and the business of Thoroughbred racing. But before these new players emerged to take part in the game the Brethren had briefly played alone, tragedy struck the world of popular music.

Late in the evening of December 8, 1980, former Beatle and international icon John Lennon was shot and killed by a crazed fan outside his Manhattan home at the Dakota. Located at Seventy-second Street and Central Park West, the luxury apartment building had originally been financed by Edward Clark, Robert Sterling Clark's grandfather, and Sterling himself had spent much of his childhood in the family's apartment there. Lennon's murderer ensured that there would never be a reunion of the four original Beatles—John, Paul, George, and Pete—who had returned from Hamburg in 1962 ready to conquer the world. But Pete Best could take some solace in the fact that he, along with his mother Mona, the horse she pawned her jewelry to bet on, and all the humans responsible for Never Say Die's surprise Derby victory had made their contributions to the most commercially successful and critically acclaimed musical group in history.

The following June at Epsom, a colt owned by Aga Khan IV named Shergar won the 202nd Derby Stakes in dominating fashion by a still-record ten lengths as the odds-on favorite. Peter Bromley, racing commentator for the BBC, declared, "There's only one horse in it. You'll need a telescope to see the rest," as Shergar cantered across the finish line.[20] Nineteen-year-old jockey Walter "the Choirboy" Swinburn won his first of three Derbies that day. Following the race, Swinburn explained, "Riding Shergar feels like riding Pegasus." Second-place jockey, journeyman John Matthias, had been excited to reach what he thought was the front of the pack in the final straightaway. "I told myself I'd achieved my life's ambition," he said. "Only then did I discover that there was another horse on the horizon."[21]

Shergar would be the last horse to win the race without the influence of an American-based stallion in his pedigree. For those who still harbored hopes of preserving the English-Irish heritage of the breed without the "taint" of American equine blood, Shergar appeared to be the last, best chance.[22] Armed with some new cash from a recent syndication deal, the Coolmore team hoped to land the record-setting colt for their stallion band.

Only months before Shergar's Derby, Robert Sangster and partners had been favored to win the big race with their undefeated two-year-old champion Storm Bird, a son of Northern Dancer they had purchased as a yearling for $1 million at the Keeneland sales. But in the winter after Storm Bird's stellar two-year-old season, a disgruntled former groom robbed the horse of his spirit under the cover of darkness. He sneaked in to O'Brien's Ballydoyle training yard in County Tipperary and cut off the colt's mane and most of his tail. Storm Bird was never the same after the cruel attack. The colt missed the Derby; raced only once more, unsuccessfully; and was retired.

Despite the setback, Storm Bird's two-year-old form and pedigree made him a marketable stallion prospect. John Magnier was soon contacted by an upstart central Kentucky operation that wanted to buy Storm Bird to stand at its Ashford Farm in Woodford County. After tense negotiations, the parties agreed to a syndication that valued Storm Bird at $28 million, an unheard-of sum at the time. The Brethren were sorry to miss the opportunity to stand the colt at Coolmore in Ireland, but again, they were presented with numbers they could not refuse. Under the agreement, the Coolmore team kept ten (of forty) shares in the stallion and would collect three annual payments of $7 million.

Flush with these new assets, the Coolmore team approached the Aga Khan in hopes of buying his Derby-winning colt Shergar to stand at their stud farm in Ireland. Shergar's European bloodlines would be a nice contrast and complement to the pedigrees of their equine stock, which was increasingly American influenced. But the Aga Khan turned them down. The world-class colt was sent instead to the Aga Khan's Ballymany Stud in County Kildare, where he stood only one season. The following winter, just days before the start of what would have been Shergar's second year at stud, the stallion was taken from his stall at Ballymany while the head groom was held at gunpoint. The groom was thrown into a car and released a few miles down the road, but Shergar was never found after his syndicate owners refused ransom demands that started at 2 million pounds. Speculation in the years since the heist has been that the Irish Republican Army was somehow involved, though critics of that theory point out that the IRA would have been unlikely to target a horse considered an Irish national hero by many. No remains or concrete explanations have ever been uncovered.

Meanwhile, a new group had emerged to challenge the Brethren in their quest to acquire the top equine prospects at the American yearling sales: Sheikh Mohammed bin Rashid Al Maktoum and his brothers, from the ruling family of Dubai. Armed with massive amounts of cash from recently discovered oil fields in their homeland, the Maktoums had supplanted the Coolmore team as the leading buyer at the Keeneland sales in 1981, with outlays totaling $9.7 million for fifteen yearlings. Included in that year's purchases was Shareef Dancer, for whom the Maktoums paid $3.3 million. The colt had a pedigree to match his price tag: his sire was Northern Dancer, and his maternal grandsire was Sir Ivor. Shareef Dancer lived up to his billing on the racetrack, winning the 1983 Irish Derby. Upon retirement, he was syndicated for a whopping $40 million, but unlike other recently syndicated stallions, Shareef Dancer was not shipped to the United States. Instead, he remained in Britain at Sheikh Mohammed's Dalham Hall Stud near Newmarket.[23]

What struck observers as quite a spending spree by the Maktoums would prove to be a mere drop in the proverbial bucket compared to what the brothers from Dubai would spend in the

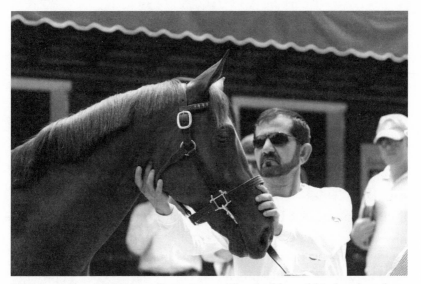

Sheikh Mohammed inspecting a horse. The sheikh and his brothers have spent well over $1 billion on Thoroughbreds. (Photos by Z)

coming years. Sheikh Mohammed had fallen in love with the sport of horse racing as a student in England and was prepared to go to any lengths necessary to build the world's leading Thoroughbred operation. The Arabian roots of the breed made the quest especially significant to him, and in 1983 Maktoum outlasted the Brethren in an epic bidding war for a son of Northern Dancer. The final bid was $10.2 million for the yearling, later named Snaafi Dancer, which would never race and would prove to be infertile. The eight-figure price for a yearling horse shocked the Thoroughbred world. As evidence, the scoreboard in the Keeneland sales pavilion was not equipped to handle a $10 million bid (the designers having assumed that seven figures would be sufficient to display any conceivable bid). The following year the Maktoums spent $51 million at Keeneland alone—more than the entire sale had grossed only five years earlier. "In the beginning," Sheikh Mohammed later recalled, "we had no horses, so we needed to buy as many as possible and we spent whatever it took, sometimes too much. We needed to set a foundation, and we did."[24]

In one sense, the Maktoums' approach to racing and breeding resembled that of European aristocrats of a century earlier, in that they seemed to have little concern for the financial return on their "investment" in racehorses. Sheikh Mohammed and his brothers simply wanted to own the very best Thoroughbreds in the world, and they would eventually spend well over $1 billion in pursuit of that goal. They also wanted to win the world's most prestigious races—not merely for monetary gain or to create stallion prospects, but for sport's sake and in the hope of bringing glory and respect to their homeland. But they were operating in an environment that was markedly changed from the one European aristocrats had dominated a century earlier. The Thoroughbred industry was big business by the 1980s, and although profit was not the primary concern of the Maktoums, they were competing on the racetrack and in the sales ring with men for whom it was. In one sense, the Maktoums were a throwback to a bygone era, but in another sense, that only underscored the more significant fact that the game had changed.

At the height of a period of unprecedented growth in the American bloodstock markets and enthusiasm for the international trend in the Thoroughbred industry, John R. Gaines, a leading Kentucky breeder and heir to a pet food fortune, announced a vision that would revolutionize the sport of horse racing: an international championship day of racing to be held each fall in the United States. Gaines had been a major player in the rush to import top European racehorses to stand in the United States,[25] and he recognized that horse racing was the only major American sport lacking a championship event to culminate its season. He also saw how successful international events, such as the Washington D.C. International Stakes and the Arlington Million, could be in drawing top European horses to America.[26]

Gaines's vision became a reality in 1984 with the first run-

John Gaines stood top European runners as stallions at his Gainesway Farm near Lexington and created the Breeders' Cup, the American year-end championship racing program. (Courtesy of University of Kentucky Archives)

ning of the Breeders' Cup, a series of seven championship-caliber races.[27] At the time, the event was billed as the richest day in all of sports, and it was a success from the beginning, drawing top horses from North America and Europe. The Breeders' Cup would later be expanded to encompass two days and fourteen races, but the basic format did not change. With the exception of the Triple Crown, no event in American racing receives as much fanfare as the Breeders' Cup, which has spawned a bevy of other international events in Japan, Hong Kong, Singapore, and, most notably, Dubai.

In 1974, the year before the Coolmore group entered the Kentucky yearling market, Keeneland's July yearling sales grossed

$17.1 million, for an average of $53,489 per yearling. By 1979, the year prior to the Maktoums' first appearance as major buyers, the Brethren had helped boost the gross to $42.4 million, for a $155,567 average. In 1984 the gross ballooned to $175.9 million, or an average of $544,681 per yearling. Kentucky breeders could hardly believe their good fortune. Lexington had become a playground for the wealthy, particularly during the summer sales, when farms lavishly entertained prospective buyers and hangers-on. *Lifestyles of the Rich and Famous* filmed a segment in Lexington during the high times and reported, "This must be what it was like before the crash in '29. Everybody's happy, there are no problems."[28]

But to the two operations most responsible for the unprecedented bloodstock bubble in the Bluegrass State, there was clearly a problem. The Coolmore team's plan to buy every potential stallion as a yearling would no longer be possible in light of the emergence of their competitors from Dubai, and they accepted an invitation to meet with Sheikh Mohammed in the spring of 1985 to discuss the situation. The details of their discussion were never made public, but upon its conclusion, Mohammed put some horses into training with Vincent O'Brien, and Robert Sangster never entered into another bidding war with the sheikh, to the great chagrin of Kentucky breeders, who had been the beneficiary of the two men's mammoth but short-lived rivalry.[29]

In 1985 Sangster and his partners paid an eye-popping $13.1 million for the half brother of American Triple Crown winner Seattle Slew by Nijinsky. With the Maktoums watching from the proverbial sidelines, Sangster outlasted a group that included Texas oilman L. R. French, former San Diego Chargers owner Eugene Klein, and American trainer D. Wayne Lukas in a furious bidding war that reached astronomical levels. Although the horse, later named Seattle Dancer, would win two stakes races and go on to a useful if unremarkable stud career, he would fail to live up to his purchase price, though in fairness to the horse,

Seattle Dancer—the son of English Triple Crown winner Nijinsky and a half brother of American Triple Crown champion Seattle Slew—attracted a world-record final bid of $13.1 million at the Keeneland yearling sale in July 1985. (Photos by Z)

only a small handful of Thoroughbreds in history would have justified such an outlay. (Sangster's world-record expenditure for an unraced colt would not be surpassed until 2006, when Coolmore associates—which did not include Sangster, who would die in 2004—outbid Sheikh Mohammed and paid $16 million for a two-year-old colt that would be named the Green Monkey and would never win a race.)

Despite the record-setting price for Seattle Dancer, the 1985 Keeneland sales declined in both gross and average from the previous year, and the American bloodstock market began a period of downturn that would last for the rest of the decade. The bubble had burst. As for Robert Sangster, his three-year reign atop the list of leading owners in England ended in 1985, when Sheikh Mohammed took over the title. The Maktoums would simply dominate British racing for the next quarter century.

In 1986 Mohammed chartered a Concorde and hosted a group of political, business, and equine industry leaders from Kentucky. The gesture was aimed at convincing the Kentuckians that his intentions were good. The group toured Dubai's nascent equine facilities, which included Nad al Sheba racecourse. Beginning in 1996, Nad al Sheba would be the site of the Dubai World Cup, the richest day of horse racing on the planet, with purses in excess of $25 million. In 2010 construction on the $1.25 billion Meydan racecourse was completed, and the Dubai World Cup was contested at its new home for the first time. The day was capped by the world's first $10 million race.[30] That Dubai would host the greatest day in racing was only fitting, Mohammed believed, because of the Arabian roots of the Thoroughbred breed.[31] He hoped that hosting such world-class events would help boost the visibility of Dubai, which he planned to position as a center of commerce and entertainment at the crossroads of Europe and Asia.

In the mid-1980s the Maktoums established bluegrass breeding bases at Gainsborough and Shadwell Farms, and over

Sheikh Mohammed is arguably the most successful and influential owner in the long history of Thoroughbred racing. (Photos by Z)

the next two decades they would acquire thousands of central Kentucky acres. Coolmore also acquired Kentucky acreage, albeit in a much more unusual manner. The partnership behind Ashford Farm, which had purchased Storm Bird from the Brethren, fell on hard times and was unable to make the second payment of $7 million. Under the terms of the agreement, ownership of the stallion reverted to Coolmore, but Ashford was not released from its monetary obligations. In lieu of cash payment, Coolmore accepted Ashford Farm itself, a state-of-the-art facility in Woodford County, in the heart of central Kentucky. Ashford became a sister breeding operation to Coolmore Ireland, thus establishing a multinational stallion-based empire that would eventually include an Australian division and a dual-hemisphere stallion shuttling program. The fact that one horse was considered more valuable than a farm comprising hundreds of acres of lush Kentucky bluegrass and including dozens of barns, houses, and other buildings is a useful illustration of the unfathomable heights to which the globalizing Thoroughbred industry had soared by the 1980s.

In the 1990s and 2000s Coolmore Ireland stood some of the most successful stallions in history, including American-bred Danehill and Sadler's Wells. Additionally, Coolmore stood European classic–winning stallions such as Dylan Thomas, Galileo, High Chaparral, and Rock of Gibraltar, each carrying prominent genetic influences from American bloodlines. Coolmore popularized the concept of a "shuttle stallion," which would be sent to the Southern Hemisphere to service mares after the Northern Hemisphere breeding season was finished, a process that further expanded and internationalized the Thoroughbred industry. At its Ashford division in Kentucky, Coolmore stood American classic winners such as Thunder Gulch, Lookin At Lucky, and Fusaichi Pegasus (the 2000 Kentucky Derby winner that was syndicated for a reported $60 million upon his retirement), as well as champion sire Giant's Causeway. Coolmore's world-class stallion band continues to generate enormous revenues, helping to ensure that Ireland retains a place of significance in the ultra-competitive global breeding industry.

Sheikh Mohammed gradually expanded his commercial breeding programs around the globe as well, establishing stallion centers under his Darley banner in England, Ireland, France, Australia, and Japan, in addition to an American operation based at what had been John A. Bell III's Jonabell Farm in Lexington. Mohammed's acquisition of Jonabell Farm brought the sheikh's total landholdings in central Kentucky to over 5,500 acres in 2001, and it would only grow from there.[32]

Within a decade, Mohammed's stallion band at the Jonabell location included Medaglia d'Oro, Quiet American, Elusive Quality, and Street Cry, each the sire of an American classic winner, as well as Street Sense and Bernardini, classic-winning runners in their own right. In 2008 a company headed by an associate of Sheikh Mohammed purchased Fasig-Tipton, North America's oldest and second-largest Thoroughbred auction company. Some of the most influential Thoroughbreds of the twentieth century were sold at Fasig-Tipton auctions over the course of the company's long history, including Man o' War, Raise a Native, Danzig, and American Triple Crown winner Seattle Slew.

Even as local breeding industries remain largely insular, the global nature of Coolmore and Darley has tended to reduce the significance of nationality in terms of equine bloodlines and stallion ownership. To illustrate, Darley announced in 2011 that it would be sending two of its stallions to China for the upcoming breeding season. Thoroughbred racing in the Pacific region is rooted in nineteenth-century European colonialism and remains immensely popular in Australia, New Zealand, Japan, Hong Kong, and elsewhere in Asia. But China represents a huge growth opportunity for the global racing and breeding industries. The year after Darley announced its entry into the Chinese Thoroughbred market, Coolmore revealed that it would be involved in creating a $2 billion equine center in the city of Tianjin, China.

The rivalry between these two international juggernauts, Coolmore and Darley, continues in the twenty-first century. These two stallion operations were home to the leading North American first-crop sires of 2011, Scat Daddy and Hard Spun. Scat Daddy is the son of Johannesburg, who won championships in Europe and the United States as a two-year-old for his Cool-more-associated owners. Each of these promising young sires carries the genetic influence of a 1970s English Derby winner from North America—John Galbreath's homebred Roberto for Hard Spun, and Triple Crown winner Nijinsky for Scat Daddy— as well as that of some of the Aga Khan's finest runners, including Nasrullah, the sire of Never Say Die. In addition to operating the most influential breeding operations in the world, Coolmore and Darley continue to win Europe's top races at a remarkable rate. In the past three decades, the Maktoum family and Cool-more associates have won well over 100 classic races (of the 300 contested) in England and Ireland alone, a feat that is difficult to fathom. In 2012 Camelot became only the third colt since Ni-jinsky to win the Two Thousand Guineas and the Epsom Der-by. Owned by Coolmore associates (who also won both English filly classics that year), Camelot became the record-tying fourth Epsom Derby winner sired by Coolmore stallion Montjeu, who died earlier that year.

Camelot entered the starting gate at the 2012 St. Leger Stakes as the 2–5 favorite. A victory would make the colt the first English Triple Crown winner in forty-two years. Jockey Joseph O'Brien, son of Camelot's trainer Aiden O'Brien,[33] allowed his horse to gallop comfortably along the rail near the back of the field until the race's final two furlongs. By the time O'Brien found running room and asked his horse to quicken, Sheikh Moham-med's colt Encke had opened up daylight between himself and the rest of the field. Camelot gained ground on Encke as the finish line approached but fell short by a diminishing length, to the shock of the Doncaster crowd. Encke's win gave Sheikh Mohammed his ninth St. Leger victory.

Encke was by Kingmambo, an American stallion that had won at the highest levels in France and England for his owner Stavros Niarchos, a Greek shipping magnate. Kingmambo was by Mr. Prospector, one of the most influential American sires of the twentieth century, and out of Miesque, a Kentucky-bred mare that won a number of top stakes in France but was best remembered for being the first two-time winner of a Breeders' Cup race, capturing the Breeders' Cup Mile over males in 1987 and 1988.

Today, the novelty of the American horse Never Say Die winning the Epsom Derby for an American owner seems quaint. The world has changed, and the sport of horse racing has evolved along with it. Just as American tycoons born of the Industrial Revolution once supplanted landed English aristocrats atop the Thoroughbred racing and breeding hierarchy, multinational operations such as Coolmore and Darley have supplanted American industrialists. But the influence of American owners and breeders who, armed with their industrial fortunes, transformed the Thoroughbred breed and industry in the twentieth century is permanent. As the industry becomes even more international and globalized, the movement of top Thoroughbred stallions will continue to serve as an indicator of economic power, just as it did in the twentieth century when top European sires and bloodlines were acquired by wealthy American horsemen, ushering in the modern era of the sport of kings.

In one sense, the increasingly commercialized nature of the global Thoroughbred racing and breeding industries is at odds with the idea of "sport," which, at its essence, is the very antithesis of serious business. But in another sense, the primary objective of anyone who chooses to participate in horse racing at any level is relatively simple and has not changed since the sport's early days: to breed and race the fastest horses possible in order to win top prizes like the Epsom Derby. Leaders of the turf from Sir Charles Bunbury to the Aga Khan, from Robert Sangster to Sheikh Mohammed, have won England's great race. But that prize is still available to anyone with a horse and a dream (or a bit of money for a wager), not just to aristocrats and royalty. Never Say Die reminded the racing world that it was possible for an American horse with an American owner to take on and defeat Europe's best three-year-olds. Along the way, he helped change the landscape of an entire sport and even made it possible for an English housewife, in her own small way, to influence the course of Western culture.

Acknowledgments

The person most responsible for this book's existence is my father, Joe Browne Nicholson. He was listening to the car radio while driving one day and happened to hear an interview of Pete Best on NPR. When Dad heard the former Beatle mention Never Say Die and the unwitting contribution the colt had made to the formation of the Beatles, he nearly stopped the car. He had heard the tale of the Derby-winning colt's birth many times from his father-in-law, my grandfather, John A. Bell III. But Dad had never heard Pete Best's story (and it's possible he had never even heard of Pete Best). To his credit, Dad did not simply make a mental note of what was a fascinating story. Instead, he made an effort to get in touch with Pete, who, as luck would have it, was scheduled to play a concert in Lexington at the now-defunct music club on Main Street called The Dame. I knew the club well, having played there regularly around the time of Pete's appearance. Dad arranged a tour for Pete and his band of Hamburg Place, the farm where Never Say Die was born, including a visit to the very stall where the newborn colt's life was saved by the timely administration of whiskey. Dad swears he saw Pete shed a tear on the "hallowed" site. In addition to my father, there are many other people to thank for helping to make this book a reality.

Everyone at the University Press of Kentucky was tremendously helpful in bringing this project to fruition. Anne Dean Watkins, Mack McCormick, Bailey Johnson, Cameron Ludwick, Ashley Runyon, Allison Webster, David Cobb, and Steve Wrinn were especially encouraging and accommodating.

Acknowledgments

I had plenty of assistance in gathering and procuring the images that appear in these pages. Benny Bell and the Bell Group in Versailles, Kentucky, were especially helpful in locating and formatting photos. Claiborne Farm's willingness to allow its photos to be published is much appreciated. Jason Flahardy at the University of Kentucky, Cathy Schenck at the Keeneland Library, and Teresa O'Toole at the Sterling and Francine Clark Art Institute were also very accommodating.

A group of friends that included Gatewood Bell, Quin Bell, Zack Bray, Alex Bushell, Ki Moon, and Walt Robertson listened to me recount the colorful story of Isaac Singer as we walked the streets of Manhattan the day before the 2011 Belmont Stakes. They feigned sufficient interest to convince me to continue my research on the subject.

My bandmates and brothers in music, Dan Carman, Justin Drury, Mark Hoffman, Barrett Milner, and Wilson Sebastian, have given me much laughter and respite from the solitudes of research and writing for many years.

Ed Bowen, Jessica Bell, and Maryjean Wall read early drafts of this book and made helpful suggestions, as did an anonymous reader provided by the publisher. James Claypool put me in contact with Nigel Sutcliffe and Timothy Cox in England, who also offered encouragement. And Linda Lotz's expert editing made this a much more readable book. The many contributions great and small from people both acknowledged and left nameless here have substantially improved this project, but its flaws are my own responsibility.

Finally, my wife, Maegan, continues to unflinchingly support me in everything I do. I am grateful she is part of my life.

Notes

1. A Historic Derby Triumph and a Wager
That Changed History

1. Roger Mortimer, *The History of the Derby Stakes* (London: Cassell, 1962), 1.

2. Edward Moorhouse, *The History and Romance of the Derby* (London: Biographical Press, 1911), 5–6; Michael Seth-Smith and Roger Mortimer, *Derby 200: The Official Story of the Blue Riband of the Turf* (Enfield, U.K.: Guinness Superlatives, 1979), 12.

3. Muriel Lennox, *Dark Horse: Unraveling the Mystery of Nearctic* (Toronto: Beach House Books, 2001), 72.

4. Lester Piggott and Sean Magee, *Lester's Derbys* (London: Methuen, 2004), 28.

5. Iroquois was bred by Aristides Welch, the man for whom the winner of the first Kentucky Derby was named, and was owned by American tobacco manufacturer Pierre Lorillard IV. Americans had won the Epsom Derby since Lorillard, including Tammany Hall power broker Richard "Boss" Croker in 1907 with Orby and Herman B. Duryea in 1914 with Durbar. But Orby had been bred in Ireland, and Durbar in France. William Collins Whitney had also won the Derby in 1901 with Volodyovski, a British horse he had leased for racing purposes. Interestingly, Durbar was sent to Claiborne Farm in Kentucky in 1924, following an early trend of top European runners being acquired for stallion duty in America.

6. Frank Jennings, "You, Too, May Win an Epsom Derby," *Thoroughbred Record*, June 12, 1954, 7.

7. Ibid. Interestingly, in the wake of Iroquois's 1881 Epsom Derby victory, similar predictions had been proffered.

8. "Upperville's Never Say Die Wins Derby in England," *Washington Post*, June 3, 1954.

9. Humphrey S. Finney, *Fair Exchange: Recollections of a Life with Horses* (London: J. A. Allen, 1974), 68.

10. Roag Best with Pete Best and Rory Best, *The Beatles: True Beginnings* (New York: St. Martin's Press, 2003), 16.

11. Pete Best and Patrick Doncaster, *Beatle: The Pete Best Story* (New York: Dell, 1985), 15–16. It was Paul McCartney's knowledge of the chords and the words to Eddie Cochran's "Twenty Flight Rock" that reportedly convinced John Lennon to allow McCartney to join the Quarrymen.

12. Ibid., 16.

13. The band's name was often written as two words—the Quarry Men—and historians have spelled it both ways. I have chosen to use one word, in large part because the surviving members of the band (they still play) insist that this is correct, according to the band's official website.

14. A group called the Les Stewart Quartet, which included Harrison and Brown, had been booked for the gig, but Stewart backed out only days before the club's opening after an argument with Brown. Harrison told Brown that he had "two mates" (Lennon and McCartney) with whom he had been playing. Perhaps, he suggested, the show could be salvaged. They pitched their solution to Mona Best, who agreed to place the Quarrymen at the top of the opening-night bill.

15. Peter Ames Carlin, *Paul McCartney: A Life* (New York: Touchstone Books, 2009), 47.

16. Ibid., 48.

17. Best, *The Beatles*, 4.

18. Bob Spitz, *The Beatles: The Biography* (New York: Little, Brown, 2005), 165.

19. Jonathan Gould, *Can't Buy Me Love: The Beatles, Britain, and America* (New York: Harmony Books, 2007), 73. Other sources claim that Sutcliffe received slightly more for that painting. See, for example, Barry Miles, *Paul McCartney: Many Years from Now* (London: Secker and Warburg, 1997), 50, and Howard Sounes, *Fab: An Intimate Life of Paul McCartney* (Cambridge, MA: Da Capo Press, 2010), 29.

20. Spencer Leigh, *The Beatles in Hamburg: The Stories, the Scene and How It All Began* (Chicago: Chicago Review Press, 2011), 42.

21. Ibid., 6.

22. See Spitz, *The Beatles*, 208; Leigh, *The Beatles in Hamburg*, 78.

23. Leigh, *The Beatles in Hamburg*, 6.

24. See ibid., 69.

25. *The Beatles Anthology Vol. 1* (Apple Records, 1995).

26. Gould, *Can't Buy Me Love*, 122–23.

27. Ray Connelly, "Pete Best: The Happiest Beatle of All," *Daily Mail*, April 7, 2007.

28. Best and Doncaster, *Beatle*, 166.

29. See Spitz, *The Beatles*, 325–30; Carlin, *Paul McCartney*, 73–74; Gould, *Can't Buy Me Love*, 123–24; Peter Brown and Steven Gaines, *The Love You Make: An Insider's Story of the Beatles* (New York: McGraw-Hill, 1983), 71.

2. The Unusual Origins of a Sewing Machine Fortune

1. See Ruth Brandon, *A Capitalist Romance: Singer and the Sewing Machine* (Philadelphia: J. B. Lippincott, 1977), 8–10.

2. Ibid., 17–18.

3. Ibid., 22.

4. Ibid., 23.

5. Don Bissel, *The First Conglomerate: 145 Years of the Singer Sewing Machine Company* (Brunswick, ME: Audenreed Press, 1999), 14.

6. J. H. Lerow and S. C. Blodgett improved on the shuttle in Howe's machine.

7. Brandon, *A Capitalist Romance*, 39–46.

8. Bissel, *The First Conglomerate*, 16. In August 1851 Singer (in his own name, not that of the partnership) obtained a patent for these improvements, the first of some twenty he would eventually secure. The group toyed with the idea of calling their machine the "Jenny Lind," after the Swedish opera star who, promoted by P. T. Barnum, had toured the United States the previous year to rave reviews, full houses, and enormous profits. That idea did not last long, however, and the partners soon settled on a permanent corporate moniker: Singer.

9. See Brandon, *A Capitalist Romance*, 67–72.

10. Ibid., 81. Soon after the ink dried on their agreement with Phelps, Singer and Zieber sold his former interest to a man named Barzillan Ransom for $10,000. But Ransom did not last long as a member of the partnership. Singer soon managed to bully and exasperate him

into selling out in exchange for forty sewing machines (which were selling for around $125 apiece).

11. Nicholas Fox Weber, *The Clarks of Cooperstown: Their Singer Sewing Machine Fortune, Their Great and Influential Art Collections, Their Forty-Year Feud* (New York: Alfred A. Knopf, 2007), 21; Brandon, *A Capitalist Romance*, 81.

12. Brandon, *A Capitalist Romance*, 85–86.

13. Stephen Birmingham, *Life at the Dakota: New York's Most Unusual Address* (New York: Random House, 1979), 25; Bissel, *The First Conglomerate*, 149.

14. Brandon, *A Capitalist Romance*, 85.

15. Bissel, *The First Conglomerate*, 47; Brandon, *A Capitalist Romance*, 116.

16. Weber, *The Clarks of Cooperstown*, 125–26.

17. See Birmingham, *Life at the Dakota*, 27–28. "The great importance of the sewing machine," one Singer brochure explained, "is in its influence upon the home; in the countless hours it has added to women's leisure for rest and refinement; in the increase of time and opportunity for that early training of children, for lack of which so many pitiful wrecks are strewn along the shores of life."

18. Birmingham, *Life at the Dakota*, 29.

19. Bissel, *The First Conglomerate*, 19; Weber, *The Clarks of Cooperstown*, 25.

20. Brandon, *A Capitalist Romance*, 156.

21. See George Washington Walling, *Recollections of a New York Chief of Police* (New York: Claxton Book Concern, 1887), 329.

22. The daughter was named Alice Eastwood Merritt, employing the surname Isaac Singer had used in his acting days.

23. Weber, *The Clarks of Cooperstown*, 27–28.

24. Bissel, *The First Conglomerate*, 40.

25. "Singer the Sewer," *Chicago Tribune*, May 9, 1875, 5.

26. "The Singer Manufacturing Company: A Vast and Wonderful Organization," *New York Times*, January 1, 1886, 4.

27. Oldway was redesigned by Singer's son Paris to resemble the Palace of Versailles. Today it is open to the public.

28. Bissel, *The First Conglomerate*, 21.

29. Weber, *The Clarks of Cooperstown*, 30.

30. Ibid., 38.

3. Robert Sterling Clark

1. The acquisition of overseas empire at the dawn of the twentieth century was justified at the time as being beneficial both to American business interests and to the persons who would be "uplifted" by an American imperial presence in their homelands. Senator Albert Jeremiah Beveridge, an Indiana Republican, encapsulated the arguments of those who defended American overseas expansion. "The Philippines are ours forever," Beveridge declared in his January 1900 address to the Senate, "'territory belonging to the United States,' as the Constitution calls them. And just beyond the Philippines are China's illimitable markets. We will not retreat from either. . . . We will not abandon our opportunity in the Orient. We will not renounce our part in the mission of our race, trustee, under God, of the civilization of the world. And we will move forward to our work, not howling out regrets like slaves whipped to their burdens, but with gratitude for a task worthy of our strength, and thanksgiving to almighty God that he has marked us as His chosen people, henceforth to lead in the regeneration of the world." Though the American push for overseas territory was new, the remainder of Beveridge's long speech—which included such choice lines as "The Pacific is our ocean," "The Filipinos are a barbarous race," and "This is the divine mission of America"—echoed themes that had been part of the story of America since the first colonial settlements in Massachusetts and Virginia: economic opportunity and godly purpose. (See *Congressional Record*, 56 Cong., 1st sess., 704–12.)

2. Nicholas Fox Weber, *The Clarks of Cooperstown: Their Singer Sewing Machine Fortune, Their Great and Influential Art Collections, Their Forty-Year Feud* (New York: Alfred A. Knopf, 2007), 114.

3. Ibid., 118.

4. Ibid., 150.

5. Ibid., 171–72.

6. Robert Sterling Clark Diary, January 16, 1929, Sterling and Francine Clark Papers, Sterling and Francine Clark Art Institute, Williamsburg, MA, cited in Weber, *The Clarks of Cooperstown*, 173.

7. Some historians have referred to the Godolphin Arabian as the Godolphin Barb (short for Barbary Coast). It is now believed that the Godolphin was of Arabian ancestry. His sire line is represented today by two-time American champion Tiznow.

8. Paul Anbinder, ed., *English, Irish, and Scottish Silver at the Sterling and Francine Clark Art Institute* (New York: Hudson Hills Press, 1997), 88. Later that year, Current added a win in the Breeders' Futurity Stakes at the Kentucky Association track in Lexington. Her winning time equaled the course record, and the field included the horse that would go on to win the Kentucky Derby the following spring, Clyde Van Dusen.

9. Weber, *The Clarks of Cooperstown*, 176.

10. Ibid., 177.

11. David Cannadine, *Mellon: An American Life* (New York: Alfred A. Knopf, 2007), 413.

12. Ibid., 314.

13. See Weber, *The Clarks of Cooperstown*, 185–205.

14. "A Plot without Plotters," *Time*, December 3, 1934.

15. Thomas M. Bancroft Jr., *The Red Polka Dots* (Easton, PA: Pinters' Printers, 2003), 55.

16. Ibid.

17. Patrick Robinson and Nick Robinson, *Horsetrader: Robert Sangster and the Rise and Fall of the Sport of Kings* (London: HarperCollins, 1994), xxi.

18. Humphrey S. Finney, *Fair Exchange: Recollections of a Life with Horses* (London: J. A. Allen, 1974), 65.

19. Ibid., 67. Timeform's *Racehorses of 1953* (Halifax, U.K.: Timeform, 1954), claims that Singing Grass won seven races, "mostly at 1¼ miles." The Internet database pedigreequerey.com has Singing Grass's career record as seven wins, four second-place finishes, and four third-place finishes in eighteen starts, including runner-up in the 1947 Falmouth Handicap in England. *Blood-Horse* claims she made nineteen career starts but credits her with only four wins.

4. The Aga Khan

1. Sultan Muhammad Shah, the Third Aga Khan, *The Memories of Aga Khan: World Enough and Time* (London: Cassell, 1954), 7.

2. See Willi Frischauer, *The Aga Khans* (London: Bodley Head, 1970), 33–37.

3. Ibid., 36.

4. As the Aga Khan grew into his position of authority, he be-

came a more visible and vocal leader of his people. In response to the violence and disease that was killing Indians by the thousands outside the confines of the palace, the Aga Khan implored his followers not to participate in sectarian violence, and he allowed himself to be publicly inoculated in an attempt to assuage fears of the practice.

5. Aga Khan, *Memories of Aga Khan*, 26.

6. Michael Nelson, *Queen Victoria and the Discovery of the Riviera* (London: I. B. Tauris, 2001), 112; Aga Khan, *Memories of Aga Khan*, 41.

7. Aga Khan, *Memories of Aga Khan*, 45.

8. Harry J. Greenwall, *His Highness the Aga Khan: Imam of the Ismailis* (London: Cresset Press, 1952), 33.

9. Though he was constantly aware of the plight of Ismailis around the world, he retained a special concern for India. His time on the Indian Legislative Council had caused the Aga Khan to become aware of the perception that the British lacked concern for Indian interests. Additionally, he was troubled by the fact that Hindus, many of whom considered Muslims to be "untouchables," controlled the most powerful Indian political organization, the Indian National Congress. In 1906 the All-India Muslim League was founded in an attempt to address some of these issues. With the Aga Khan serving as the first president, the league soon became a political force to be reckoned with. At first the league focused on uniting Muslims and raising awareness of their plight in India, but it would later become a major player in the push for Indian independence and the creation of the nation of Pakistan. To further promote the objectives of the league, the Aga Khan traveled around the world in 1907, giving speeches and making public appearances. Upon his return, his generally poor health and a lingering case of bronchitis concerned his doctors, who endorsed his decision to recuperate in the friendly climes of Monte Carlo. While in Africa on official business in 1905, the Aga Khan was disturbed by the conditions of an Ismaili community he visited, including a high incidence of tuberculosis, laziness, and lax attention to religion. He decided to draft a written constitution for Ismailis everywhere, the first of its kind for his people. The document that emerged condemned the mistreatment of women, child marriage, polygamy, and all-male education, while calling for increased efforts to promote health and sanitation. The most severe penalty for violation of the constitution was excommunication.

The Aga Khan also helped establish a hierarchy of provincial and local councils that would be led by locally nominated leaders.

10. Ecstatic to have a male heir, the Aga Khan traveled extensively that year to visit his followers and meet with heads of state regarding Ismaili populations in various lands. He visited Turkey and met with Sultan Mohammed V, who had been chosen to replace his deposed brother in the wake of the Young Turk Revolution. There, the Aga Khan found an impotent sultanate and a menacing German hand meddling in domestic affairs. He knew that in times of disturbance and upheaval, his traditionally nomadic people faced bodily harm and displacement. With the possibility of widespread war in and around Europe already beginning to loom, the Aga Khan was rightly concerned about what might happen to his people in the event of protracted instability.

11. In a private moment, King George told the Aga Khan of his intention to become the first reigning British monarch to visit India that winter to celebrate his coronation with his subjects in the jewel of the British Empire. The king's true motivation for the journey was a desire to quell the nascent nationalist movement there and to shore up support for the Crown, but the prospect of a visit from the monarch excited the Aga Khan.

12. The imam sent letters and telegrams and made phone calls and personal visits to influential Muslims around the world, making the case that Britain's allies could protect Turkish interests from Russian threats and that it would be in Turkey's best interest to remain neutral while the European powers weakened themselves at war. Though the Turks remained allied with Germany, their calls for jihad were ultimately ignored. Next, the Aga was dispatched to Egypt, where he was asked to help shore up support for the British cause there. He appealed to the professors at Al-Azhar University, one of the world's leading Islamic institutes of higher learning, arguing that if the Germans prevailed, their tyrannical attitudes toward governance would not be good for Muslims.

13. Aga Khan, *Memories of Aga Khan*, 196.

14. Greenwall, *His Highness the Aga Khan*, xi.

15. See Aga Khan, *Memories of Aga Khan*, 194–99. Lambton introduced the Aga Khan to Irish trainer Richard "Dick" Dawson and recommended that the Aga hire him to train his British stock. Lambton

also recommended William Duke, whom the imam knew well, to train for him in France. William K. Vanderbilt, who had a string of horses with Duke, had introduced the Aga Khan to the trainer almost twenty years before. Vanderbilt, the grandson of railroad magnate "Commodore" Cornelius Vanderbilt, had been an early member of the powerful Jockey Club in New York City before moving to France, where he achieved marked success as a racehorse owner and breeder. He had taken a liking to the Aga Khan in the years before the war and had shown the imam all he knew about the administration of a top-level racing operation. Vanderbilt also made sure the Aga Khan had an open invitation to visit Duke's training yard near Deauville, where Duke taught the Aga some of the nuances of Thoroughbred breeding and conformation evaluation. Vanderbilt's death in 1920 had freed up some stable space, allowing Duke to accept a new major client, and he agreed to take on a string of horses for the Aga Khan. The partnership quickly bore fruit: a colt named Pot au Feu won the French Derby in 1924. Duke, an American, returned to the United States the following year. But the seeds of what would become the Aga Khan's three decades of dominance of European racing had already been sown.

5. Robber Barons Robbing Barons

1. Marshall Smith, "The People's Horse," *Life Magazine*, September 21, 1953.

2. Alan Yuill Walker, *Grey Magic: The Enigma of the Grey Thoroughbred* (Compton, U.K.: Highdown, 2005), 227.

3. Ibid., 231.

4. Ibid., 130.

5. His other top runners that year included Diophon and Salmon-Trout, winners of the first and last legs of the English Triple Crown, respectively, the Two Thousand Guineas and the St. Leger.

6. *American Racing Manual 1954* (New York: Daily Racing Form, 1953), 1144.

7. Edward L. Bowen, *Dynasties: Great Thoroughbred Stallions* (Lexington, KY: Eclipse Press, 2000), 61.

8. Edward L. Bowen, *Legacies of the Turf: A Celebration of Great Thoroughbred Breeders*, vol. 1 (Lexington, KY: Eclipse Press, 2003), 63.

9. William H. P. Robertson, *The History of Thoroughbred Racing in America* (Englewood Cliffs, NJ: Prentice-Hall, 1964), 38.

10. B. G. Bruce, "Memoir of Lexington," *Kentucky Live Stock Record*, December 4, 1880.

11. Meddler was the sire of the dam of 1914 Epsom Derby winner Durbar, whose bottom-line female family were all American bred, back to Black Selima—daughter of Selima, herself a daughter of the Godolphin Arabian. Durbar was not considered a purebred under the Jersey Act and stood as a stallion in France until 1924, when he was imported to America to stand at Claiborne Farm.

12. See Bowen, *Dynasties*, 41–46.

13. Sultan Muhammad Shah, the Third Aga Khan, *The Memories of Aga Khan: World Enough and Time* (London: Cassell, 1954), 221–28.

14. Muriel Lennox, *Dark Horse: Unraveling the Mystery of Nearctic* (Toronto: Beach House Books, 2001), 97.

15. Ibid.

16. Gubblini had learned from a bad experience in the same race the previous year, when French jockeys had combined to restrict his movement on Donatello.

17. Aga Khan, *Memories of Aga Khan,* 221–28.

18. *American Racing Manual 1954*, 1144.

19. *Sports Illustrated*, November 1, 1954.

20. Paul Mathiu, *The Masters of Manton: From Alec Taylor to George Todd* (London: Write First Time, 2010), 162.

21. Phil Bull, *Best Racehorses of 1943* (London: Portway Press, 1944), 156.

22. Bowen, *Dynasties*, 120. Although the historical record is conflicted, it appears that Nasrullah was purchased upon his retirement from racing by Gerald McElligott and Bert Kerr, doing business as "Nasrullah Syndicate." That pair then sold him to McGrath for approximately $75,000. See Bowen, *Dynasties*, 252. McGrath would win the Epsom Derby as an owner with Irish-bred Arctic Prince, who stood four seasons as a stallion in England before being exported to the United States.

23. Bowen, *Dynasties*, 117. *American Racing Manual 1954* lists Nasrullah's syndication value at $372,000.

24. In 2011 Noor's remains were reinterred at Old Friends Thor-

oughbred retirement facility in Georgetown, Kentucky, after it was discovered that his burial site in California was going to be developed as condominiums.

25. Bowen, *Dynasties*, 121.

26. Nicholas Clee, *Eclipse: The Story of the Rogue, the Madam, and the Horse That Changed Racing* (London: Bantam Press, 2010), 157.

6. An Unlikely Horseman

1. Len Tracy, "Yankee Victory," *Thoroughbred Record*, June 12, 1954, 8.

2. Ibid., 9.

3. No one would be more influential in the American steel industry than a diminutive immigrant named Andrew Carnegie, born in Dunfermline, Scotland, in 1835. He came to America as a boy with his parents and became one of the wealthiest men in history, helping to build, literally and figuratively, the modern United States. Upon his arrival in the Pittsburgh area in 1848, Carnegie immediately went to work, first in a cotton mill and later as a telegraph messenger and operator. Step by step, he built a corporate empire whose crown jewel would be Carnegie Steel Company, which he sold to J. Pierpont Morgan in 1901 in a deal that made Carnegie one of the richest men on earth. Upon his retirement from business affairs, Carnegie set out to give away all his money, paying special attention to the building of libraries across the country and around the world. His philanthropic interest in libraries reflected his belief that anyone could achieve worldly success if he or she had access to education. Carnegie publicized his own rags-to-riches story during his own lifetime and in a posthumously published autobiography. That story served as a model for the nation in an era of extraordinary economic growth. Many wealthy American Thoroughbred owners and breeders followed a path similar to Carnegie's, but others were beneficiaries of the more time-tested model of inheritance.

4. *New York Times*, March 17, 1922.

5. *New York Times*, March 18, 1922.

6. *Chicago Tribune*, April 28, 1925.

7. *New York Times*, April 28, 1925.

8. Ibid.

9. During Bell Sr.'s trial, the old man lived in a cottage on Bell Farm; his son's family, including Bell III, lived in the milkmen's quarters.

10. *New York Times*, July 26, 1929.

11. Despite the fact that modern killing machines had all but ended the practical military use of horses in battle, the U.S. Army continued to utilize the animals on battlefields on a limited basis, even during the Second World War.

12. As a four-year-old, Discovery had generally been regarded as the horse of the year over Triple Crown champion Omaha and was one of the most accomplished handicap horses of all time.

13. Edward L. Bowen, *Masters of the Turf: Ten Trainers Who Dominated Horse Racing's Golden Age* (Lexington, KY: Eclipse Press, 2007), 135.

14. Ibid., 137.

15. Ibid., 139.

16. Ibid., 142.

17. McCreary was an interesting figure whose varied political career spanned parts of six decades and revealed much about the ebb and flow of American politics of the era. He was born in Richmond, Kentucky, in 1838, graduated from Centre College in nearby Danville, and then earned a law degree from Cumberland College in Tennessee. He was practicing law in his hometown when the Civil War began, so he joined a local Confederate Army regiment and was given a commission. He participated in a raid of Ohio led by General John Hunt Morgan and was eventually captured. McCreary resumed his law practice after the war and entered politics in 1869, gaining election to Kentucky's House of Representatives (where he eventually became speaker) in part because of his Confederate war record. In 1875 he was elected governor of Kentucky. McCreary had defeated three other former Confederate soldiers for the Democratic nomination and then beat Republican John Marshall Harlan, a former Union soldier (Harlan, as a Supreme Court justice, would cast the only dissenting vote in the notorious *Plessy v. Ferguson* decision that endorsed "separate but equal" accommodations for blacks and whites). Following his first stint as governor, McCreary again returned to his law practice in Richmond. He was elected to the first of six congressional terms in 1884 and later served as a U.S. senator; in 1911, at the age of seventy-three, he was elected governor of Kentucky for the

second time. Though he had been a "Bourbon" Democrat for most of his political life, he ran for governor as a Progressive Democrat this time, advocating education reform, election reform, creation of a public utilities commission, and women's voting rights. In the late nineteenth and early twentieth centuries, part of the multifaceted spirit of progressive reform sweeping communities across the United States was directed at unfettered capitalism and big business. These reform movements led to federal laws that regulated food and drugs, child labor, and monopolies. Though widely criticized by industrial leaders, these reforms arguably prevented more radical reform and did little to hamper the expansion of what was, by that time, the world's leading industrial economy.

18. Interview with Jessica Bell and Bennett Bell Williams, September 24, 2008, Horse Industry in Kentucky Oral History Project, Louis B. Nunn Center for Oral History, University of Kentucky.

19. Kent Hollingsworth, *The Wizard of the Turf: John E. Madden of Hamburg Place* (Lexington, KY: Blood-Horse, 1965), 31.

20. Ibid.

21. Ibid., 27.

22. Ibid., 19.

23. Though Madden was hardly shy about taking credit for his successes, he ultimately acknowledged the horses themselves as the real heroes of the sport. When asked by a reporter to explain what makes a good racehorse, Madden replied, "It seems to me that nature is mainly responsible for our kings and queens of the Turf. Racehorses, like poets, are born. If I had the power to make good racehorses, I would have none but the best." Ibid., 31.

24. Ibid., 109.

25. Tracy, "Yankee Victory," 9.

26. Ibid.

27. Ibid.

28. Ibid., 19.

29. The first transatlantic airplane transportation of horses occurred in the 1940s, and by the 1950s, it was not unusual for horses to be flown from America to Europe. The historical record does not reveal how Never Say Die was transported to Europe. Given that he traveled via ship in utero, it is reasonable to assume that Clark sent his yearlings in the same manner three years later. See Whitney Tower, "Banana Nose Shows 'em How," *Sports Illustrated*, November 15, 1954.

7. A Derby-less Trainer

1. Quoted in Paul Mathiu, *The Masters of Manton: From Alec Taylor to George Todd* (London: Write First Time, 2010), 19.
2. Ibid., 68–69.
3. Ibid., 62–63.
4. From his first nine yearling purchases, Watson won the Grand Prix de Paris and the Oaks, among other stakes wins and placings.
5. Quoted in Mathiu, *Masters of Manton*, 168.
6. Ibid.

8. The First Kentucky-Bred Champion of the Epsom Derby

1. Editorial staff of Timeform, *Racehorses of 1954: Timeform Annual* (Halifax, U.K.: Timeform, 1955).
2. Lester Piggott and Sean Magee, *Lester's Derbys* (London: Methuen, 2004), 18.
3. Mercer would suffer an untimely death five years later in a racetrack spill.
4. Scobie Breasley was one of the best riders in Britain. He won four English riding titles and practically every top race in the country. He was known for his tendency to position his horses on the rail and wait as long as possible to make his move. This strategy matched Never Say Die's natural running style quite well, but it was better suited for the longer races the colt would run as a three-year-old.
5. Quoted in Piggott and Magee, *Lester's Derbys*, 16.
6. In addition to local acclaim, a bottle of champagne and a pound of local sausage were awarded to the winner of the Newmarket Town Plate each year.
7. Lester Piggott, *Lester: The Autobiography of Lester Piggott* (London: Partridge Press, 1995), 5.
8. This is not the same Davy Jones who would make a name for himself as a member of the Monkees, although the pop star worked with horses as a boy and once had aspirations of becoming a jockey.
9. Zucchero would finish third as the post-time favorite in the first running of the Washington D.C. International Stakes the following year.

10. Piggott and Magee, *Lester's Derbys*, 16.

11. Elopement was owned by eccentric bon vivant Sir Victor Sassoon, who, after his fourth Derby victory, is famously rumored to have said, "There is only one race greater than the Jews and that is the Derby." See Jonathan Fenby, *Generalissimo: Chiang Kai-shek and the China He Lost* (London: Free Press, 2003), 135.

12. Frank Jennings, "You, Too, May Win an Epsom Derby," *Thoroughbred Record*, June 12, 1954, 7.

13. Dick Francis, *A Jockey's Life: The Biography of Lester Piggott* (New York: Fawcett Crest, 1986), 55.

14. Len Tracy, "Yankee Victory," *Thoroughbred Record*, June 12, 1954, 9.

15. Piggott and Magee, *Lester's Derbys*, 21.

16. *Blood-Horse*, June 12, 1954.

17. Piggott, *Lester*, 23.

18. Tracy, "Yankee Victory," 9.

19. Piggott and Magee, *Lester's Derbys*, 29.

20. *New York Times*, September 12, 1954.

21. *Thoroughbred Record*, September 25, 1954.

22. The National Stud is a not-for-profit organization dedicated to the preservation and improvement of the Thoroughbred and to the education of the public. It got its start with a 1916 donation of land by Colonel William Hall-Walker, Lord Wavertree, one of the many highly placed Brits who had introduced the Aga Khan to English racing earlier in the century.

23. *New York Times*, May 26, 1956.

9. An American Invasion at Epsom

1. Never Say Die's offspring also included 1960 One Thousand Guineas and Oaks winner Never Too Late.

2. *Schenectady (NY) Gazette*, June 7, 1962.

3. Nicholas Schaffner, *The Beatles Forever: How They Changed Our Culture* (New York: MJF Books, 1978), 36, 51.

4. *St. Petersburg (FL) Times*, May 30, 1968.

5. Quoted in Lester Piggott and Sean Magee, *Lester's Derbys* (London: Methuen, 2004), 94.

6. *Thoroughbred Record*, June 15, 1958, 1547.

7. Quoted in Piggott and Magee, *Lester's Derbys*, 94.

8. Ibid.

9. Lester Piggott, *Lester: The Autobiography of Lester Piggott* (London: Partridge Press, 1995), 85.

10. Sir Ivor was sired by Sir Gaylord, whose half brother was American superhorse Secretariat. Sir Gaylord, in turn, was sired by Turn-to, a British-bred horse imported to America and purchased as a yearling by Harry F. Guggenheim, an influential American publisher and heir to an immense mining and smelting fortune. Alice Headley had been married to John A. Bell III's brother, Reynolds Wait "Nick" Bell, from 1950 to 1965. In 1962 she inherited part of her father's Beaumont Farm (across the road from John Bell's Jonabell Farm), where she founded Mill Ridge. Alice's father, Hal Price Headley, was one of the leading Thoroughbred breeders in Kentucky and was involved in some of the early syndication deals that brought English stallions to stand in the Bluegrass State.

11. *St. Petersburg (FL) Times*, May 30, 1968.

12. In 1923 Epsom Derby winner Papyrus traveled to the United States for a match race with Kentucky Derby winner Zev at Belmont Park in New York. Heavy rain caused the track to become deep with mud, and Zev won the race comfortably.

13. *Pittsburgh Post-Gazette*, June 4, 1970.

14. Ibid.

15. See Whitney Tower, "Saints and Sidewalks," *Sports Illustrated*, June 15, 1970. Gyr's sire, Sea-Bird II, was one of the top European runners in his day, winning the 1965 Epsom Derby and Arc de Triomphe. John W. Galbreath reportedly paid well over $1 million to lease the stallion for stud duties. He stood seven seasons at Galbreath's Darby Dan Farm before returning to France, where he died in 1972.

16. *Thoroughbred Record*, June 30, 1970, 1582. The sale was held at Taylor's Windfields Farm.

17. Piggott, *Lester*, 108.

18. *Thoroughbred Record*, June 30, 1970, 1582.

19. *Ocala (FL) Star-Banner*, June 28, 1970.

20. *St. Joseph (NY) News Press*, September 13, 1970.

21. *Calgary Herald*, October 1, 1970.

22. Whitney Tower, "Even the Very Best Can Blunder," *Sports Illustrated*, October 26, 1970.

23. "Nijinsky Will Stand in Kentucky," *Spartanburg (SC) Herald-*

Journal, August 16, 1970. Nijinsky would be registered as Nijinsky II when he was retired for stud duty in America because there was already a horse named Nijinsky registered there.

24. Ferdinand won the 1986 Kentucky Derby, and Kentucky-bred Shahrastani won the Epsom Derby that year. Nijinsky later sired 1995 Epsom Derby winner Lammtarra, raced by Sheikh Mohammed's nephew, Saeed bin Maktoum bin Rashid Al Maktoum. Lammtarra won each of his four career starts, including the Arc de Triomphe. He began his stud career at Sheikh Mohammed's Dalham Hall Stud before being sold to Japanese interests for a reported $30 million. He was later reacquired by Sheikh Mohammed and returned to England.

25. Peter Towers-Clark, "Mill Reef Flays the European Opposition," *Thoroughbred Record*, June 12, 1971. An attractive explanation for the increase in American overseas success was the wider availability of transatlantic aviation, but as an editorial in the same issue of the *Thoroughbred Record* explained, the reality was not that simple: "None of the American-bred winners of the Derby had utilized jet travel for a one-shot invasion of England. All of them were shipped over long beforehand and began their racing careers as two-year-olds in England or, in the cases of Sir Ivor and Nijinsky II, Ireland."

26. Peter Towers-Clark, "Roberto Extended the String," *Thoroughbred Record*, June 17, 1972, 1536. "Clemente just loves horses and racing, and he has a lot of quality. I wanted to name a horse for him and I wanted it to be a horse with quality," Galbreath explained.

27. Quoted in Piggott and Magee, *Lester's Derbys*, 132.

28. Ibid., 139.

29. Ibid., 140.

10. A Global Sport and Industry

1. Patrick Robinson and Nick Robinson, *Horsetrader: Robert Sangster and the Rise and Fall of the Sport of Kings* (London: HarperCollins, 1994), 66. The authors do not cite the sources of the quotations used in their book. They are included here to add a bit of color, without an endorsement as to their literal accuracy.

2. A share in a stallion is a partial ownership interest in that horse. A season is the right to breed a mare to the stallion in a given breeding season.

3. Affirmed was valued at $14.4 million for syndication purposes in 1979, and Spectacular Bid's syndication was worth a reported $22 million the following year. See "Spectacular Bid Brings Record Syndication Figure," *Fredericksburg (VA) Free Lance-Star*, March 12, 1980.

4. Robinson and Robinson, *Horsetrader*, 53.

5. *Racing Post*, May 27, 2011; *New York Times*, November 17, 1990.

6. Quoted in Lester Piggott and Sean Magee, *Lester's Derbys* (London: Methuen, 2004), 168. One hand is four inches. An average racehorse is sixteen hands tall.

7. Ibid., 169.

8. "Bunker's Busted Silver Bubble," *Time*, May 12, 1980.

9. "Bunker Hunt's Comstock Lode," *Time*, January 14, 1980. In the aftermath of Hunt's French Derby victory, Baron Guy de Rothschild, president of the French Breeders Association, allegedly initiated a push to restrict many French races to European-bred horses.

10. Youth went on to win the Washington D.C. International Stakes that year and would later sire Teenoso, winner of the 1983 Epsom Derby. Lester Piggott won his ninth and final Derby aboard Teenoso.

11. Nobiliary would go on to win the 1975 Washington D.C. International Stakes. She is the last filly to have placed in the Derby. See William Leggett, "O.K., Bring On the Boys," *Sports Illustrated*, November 17, 1975.

12. William Johnson, "Dr. Beauty Buys a Beast," *Sports Illustrated*, February 19, 1968.

13. Robinson and Robinson, *Horsetrader*, 104.

14. "Aly Khan's Son, 20, New Aga Khan," *New York Times*, July 13, 1957, 1.

15. Joe David Brown, "Beware of Women and Horses," *Sports Illustrated*, March 23, 1959.

16. Ray Cave, "A Man of Quality," *Sports Illustrated*, May 23, 1960.

17. Blushing Groom was a son of Red God, himself a lesser son of Nasrullah. The brilliant French-bred colt came from equine bloodlines of the Aga Khan's, but the mare had been culled from his broodmare band. Thus, the Aga Khan was not the breeder of Blushing Groom but bought him as a yearling. Blushing Groom would become an influential international stallion that stood in Kentucky, and his many top offspring included Nashwan, who would win the 1989 English Derby for owner Sheikh Hamdan Al Maktoum (whose family would soon chal-

lenge the Brethren's spot atop the racing world), as well as Arazi, Rahy, Candy Stripes, Rainbow Quest, and Sky Beauty.

18. Piggott and Magee, *Lester's Derbys*, 178.

19. The tantalizing possibility of running him against American Triple Crown winner Seattle Slew at the Washington D.C. International Stakes that November had also been discussed but never materialized.

20. Owen Slot, "I'll Never Forget That Night . . . the IRA Led Shergar into the Box without a Problem," *Telegraph* (London), June 2, 2001.

21. Tom Richmond, "Memories of How the Late, Great Shergar Cruised to Victory with a Wonderful Record-Breaking Display in the 1981 Epsom Derby," *Yorkshire Post*, May 30, 2011.

22. Five generations back in Shergar's pedigree, an American-bred stallion named Tracery appears. Owned and bred by August Belmont Jr., Tracery was sent to England during troubled times for New York racing. He won the St. Leger, Sussex, and St. James's Palace Stakes and was third in the Derby Stakes as a three-year-old. He won three stakes at four before entering Southcourt Stud in England. He also stood for a time in South America at the end of his career.

23. That year, the owners of Northern Dancer were rumored to have turned down a $40 million offer for the twenty-one-year-old stallion. Paul Mellon was vehemently opposed to forcing the old stud to move. See Robinson and Robinson, *Horsetrader*, 173–75.

24. Quoted in Jason Levin, *From the Desert to the Derby: The Ruling Family of Dubai's Billion-Dollar Quest to Win America's Greatest Horse Race* (New York: Daily Racing Form Press, 2002), 127.

25. Vaguely Noble, Blushing Groom, Riverman, and Lyphard were among the studs at his Gainesway Farm in Lexington.

26. The Arlington Million, first held in 1981, is a million-dollar race on the turf at Chicago's Arlington Park.

27. The seven Breeders' Cup events were the Juvenile (for two-year-old colts), the Juvenile Fillies (for two-year-old fillies), the Sprint (six furlongs on the dirt), the Mile (on the grass), the Distaff ($1\frac{1}{8}$ miles on the dirt, restricted to fillies and mares), the Turf ($1\frac{1}{2}$ miles on the grass), and the Classic ($1\frac{1}{4}$ miles on the dirt).

28. Quoted in James C. Nicholson, *The Kentucky Derby: How the Run for the Roses Became America's Premier Sporting Event* (Lexington: University Press of Kentucky, 2012), 180.

29. Clive Gammon, "Call It the Sport of Sheikhs," *Sports Illustrated*, December 1, 1986.

30. *Guardian (U.K.)*, January 28, 2010.

31. Mohammed also hoped that hosting world-class events such as the Dubai World Cup and major golf and tennis tournaments would help promote Dubai as a major tourist destination and financial and commercial center. The Maktoums had become fabulously wealthy as a result of oil production, but they knew oil is a finite resource and hoped to create a more sustainable model for economic success.

32. In a statement to the *Blood-Horse*, Sheikh Mohammed's bloodstock adviser, John Ferguson, said that Never Say Die had been among the champions raised at Jonabell Farm, citing this as evidence that the sheikh was buying top land from an established Thoroughbred operation. But Never Say Die was actually foaled and raised at acreage leased from Hamburg Place. Bell moved his operation to the Bowman's Mill Road location in 1954.

33. Aiden and Joseph O'Brien are not related to trainer Vincent O'Brien. But Aiden did train Camelot at Ballydoyle, the same facility that Vincent oversaw for so many prosperous years.

Bibliography

"Aga Khan's Colts Favored for Derby: Newmarket Suits Powerful Finishers." *Daily Racing Form*, June 4, 1943.

Alderson, Andrew. "The Truth about Shergar Racehorse Kidnapping." *Telegraph* (London), January 27, 2003.

"Aly Khan's Son, 20, New Aga Khan." *New York Times*, July 13, 1957.

American Racing Manual 1954. New York: Daily Racing Form, 1953.

Anbinder, Paul, ed. *English, Irish, and Scottish Silver at the Sterling and Francine Clark Art Institute*. New York: Hudson Hills Press, 1997.

"April the Fifth Is Surprise Winner of the Epsom Derby." *Daily Racing Form*, June 2, 1932.

Archer, Jules. *The Plot to Seize the White House*. New York: Hawthorn Books, 1973.

Aurbach, Ann Hagedorn. *Wild Ride: The Rise and Tragic Fall of Calumet Farm, Inc., America's Premiere Racing Dynasty*. New York: Henry Holt, 1994.

Bancroft, Thomas M., Jr. *The Red Polka Dots*. Easton, PA: Pinters' Printers, 2003.

"Banker Found Guilty of $600,000 Theft." *Washington Post*, December 9, 1925.

Barron, James. "Raymond Guest, 84, Ambassador, Polo Player, and Breeder of Horses." *New York Times*, January 1, 1992.

Barzini, Luigi, Jr. "The Search for a Superhorse." *Sports Illustrated*, December 10, 1956.

The Beatles. *The Beatles Anthology*. San Francisco: Chronicle, 2000.

Bell, John A. "The John Arner Bells." Unpublished manuscript in the author's possession, 2002.

"Bell out of Senate Race." *New York Times*, March 29, 1922.

"The Bell Telephone." *Boston Globe*, March 26, 1884.

Bibliography

"Bell to Enter Fight for the Senatorship: Pennsylvania Primary Contest Is Expected to Cause Republican Rift." *New York Times*, March 27, 1922.

Best, Pete, and Patrick Doncaster. *Beatle! The Pete Best Story*. New York: Dell, 1985.

Best, Pete, and Bill Harry. *The Best Years of the Beatles*. London: Headline, 1997.

Best, Roag, with Pete Best and Rory Best. *The Beatles: True Beginnings*. New York: St. Martin's Press, 2003.

"Big Deal Alleged to 'Sell' Crow's Seat: Sproul and Bell Flatly Deny a Report of $650,000 Plot in Pennsylvania." *New York Times*, March 17, 1922.

Birmingham, Stephen. *Life at the Dakota: New York's Most Unusual Address*. New York: Random House, 1979.

"Bishop Potter Will Wed Again." *Chicago Tribune*, July 13, 1902.

Bissell, Don. *The First Conglomerate: 145 Years of the Singer Sewing Machine Company*. Brunswick, ME: Audenreed Press, 1999.

Bowen, Edward L. *Bold Ruler*. Lexington, KY: Eclipse Press, 2005.

———. *Dynasties: Great Thoroughbred Stallions*. Lexington, KY: Eclipse Press, 2000.

———. *Legacies of the Turf: A Celebration of Great Thoroughbred Breeders*. Vol. 1. Lexington, KY: Eclipse Press, 2003.

———. *Legacies of the Turf: A Celebration of Great Thoroughbred Breeders*. Vol. 2. Lexington, KY: Eclipse Press, 2004.

———. *Man o' War*. Lexington, KY: Eclipse Press, 2000.

———. *Masters of the Turf: Ten Trainers Who Dominated Horse Racing's Golden Age*. Lexington, KY: Eclipse Press, 2007.

———. *Nashua*. Lexington, KY: Eclipse Press, 2003.

———. *War Admiral*. Lexington, KY: Eclipse Press, 2002.

Bowen, Edward L., et al. *10 Best Kentucky Derbies*. Lexington, KY: Eclipse Press, 2005.

Boyd, Eva Jolene Boyd. *Assault: Thoroughbred Legend*. Lexington, KY: Eclipse Press, 2004.

Bramwell, Tony, and Rosemary Kingsland. *Magical Mystery Tours: My Life with the Beatles*. New York: Thomas Dunne Books, 2005.

Brandon, Ruth. *A Capitalist Romance: Singer and the Sewing Machine*. Philadelphia: J. B. Lippincott, 1977.

"British Stud Gets '54 Derby Winner." *New York Times*, May 26, 1956.

Bibliography

Broadhead, Fred C. *Here Comes Whirlaway!* Manhattan, KS: Sunflower University Press, 1995.

"Brothers Fight Legal War over Singer Millions." *Chicago Tribune*, October 21, 1927.

Brown, Joe David. "Aly Khan: Sporting Price." *Sports Illustrated*, March 23, 1959.

———. "Beware of Women and Horses." *Sports Illustrated*, March 23, 1959.

Brown, Peter, and Steven Gaines. *The Love You Make: An Insider's Story of the Beatles*. New York: McGraw-Hill, 1983.

Browne, David. *Fire and Rain: The Beatles, Simon and Garfunkel, James Taylor, CSNY, and the Last Story of 1970*. New York: Da Capo Press, 2011.

Bruce, B. G. "Memoir of Lexington." *Kentucky Live Stock Record*, December 4, 1880.

Bull, Phil. *Best Horses of 1943*. London: Portway Press, 1944.

"Bunker Hunt's Comstock Lode." *Time*, January 14, 1980.

"Bunker's Busted Silver Bubble." *Time*, May 12, 1980.

Butler, Smedley D. *War Is a Racket*. Los Angeles: Feral House, 2003.

Cain, Glenye. *The Home Run Horse: Inside America's Billion-Dollar Racehorse Industry and the High-Stakes Dreams That Fuel It*. New York: Daily Racing Form Press, 2004.

Cannandine, David. *Mellon: An American Life*. New York: Alfred A. Knopf, 2007.

Capps, Timothy T. *Affirmed and Alydar*. Lexington, KY: Eclipse Press, 2002.

———. *Secretariat*. Lexington, KY: Eclipse Press, 2007.

———. *Spectacular Bid*. Lexington, KY: Eclipse Press, 2001.

Carlin, Peter Ames. *Paul McCartney: A Life*. New York: Touchstone Books, 2009.

Case, Carole. *The Right Blood: America's Aristocrats in Thoroughbred Racing*. New Brunswick, NJ: Rutgers University Press, 2001.

Cave, Ray. "A Man of Quality." *Sports Illustrated*, May 23, 1960.

Clark, Robert Sterling. Diary. Sterling and Francine Clark Papers, Sterling and Francine Clark Art Institute, Williamstown, MA.

"Clark's Galatea II Wins: Favorite Annexes Oaks at Epsom." *New York Times*, May 17, 1939.

Clarke, Gerald. "A Portrait of the Donor." *Time*, May 8, 1978.

Clee, Nicholas. *Eclipse: The Story of the Rogue, the Madam, and the Horse That Changed Racing.* London: Bantam Press, 2010.

Conley, Kevin. *Stud: Adventures in Breeding.* New York: Bloomsbury, 2002.

Connolly, Ray. "Pete Best, the Happiest Beatle of All." *Daily Mail,* April 7, 2007.

"Crossroads Museum: Clark Art Institute." *Time,* May 7, 1956.

"Current, E. Pool Up, Wins at Louisville: Clark Filly Leads Frances Milward by Five Lengths in the Churchill Downs Feature." *New York Times,* November 27, 1928.

"Current Equals Course Record in Winning $18,500 Futurity at Lexington." *New York Times,* November 18, 1928.

"Darius Tops Derby List: Replaces Rowston Manor as the Epsom Favorite Tomorrow." *New York Times,* June 1, 1954.

"Death on a Curve." *Time,* May 23, 1960.

"Declining Years of Once Rich Coal Men Full of Adversity." *Chicago Tribune,* January 11, 1931.

"Denouncing Deal Talk, Senator Crow May Run: Angered by Story, He Will Consult Doctors—Bell Likely to Be Rival Candidate." *New York Times,* March 18, 1922.

"Derby Choice under Guard: Elaborate Precautions Taken to Protect American-Owned Orwell, Epsom Derby Favorite." *Daily Racing Form,* May 27, 1932.

"Derby Week Brings Festivity to London." *New York Times,* May 31, 1936.

"Dog Show Draws Increasing Public: Westminster Exhibit Reveals Unexpected General Interest." *New York Times,* February 25, 1917.

Duke, Jacqueline, ed. *Thoroughbred Champions: Top 100 Racehorses of the 20th Century.* Lexington, KY: Blood-Horse, 1999.

Editorial staff of Timeform. *Racehorses of 1953: Timeform Annual.* Halifax, U.K.: Timeform, 1954.

———. *Racehorses of 1954: Timeform Annual.* Halifax, U.K.: Timeform, 1955.

Edwards, Anne. *Throne of Gold: The Lives of the Aga Khans.* New York: William Morrow, 1995.

Edwards, Willard. "Act Cautiously to Investigate Butler's Coup: Furor Causes Inquiry to Walk Softly." *Chicago Tribune,* November 22, 1934.

"English Trainer Joe Lawson Passes Away at Age 83." *Daily Racing Form*, May 20, 1963.

"Ex-Marine Head Reveals 'Wild Fascist Plan': 'Ridiculous,' Say Men Named." *Chicago Tribune*, November 21, 1934.

Fabian, Ann. *Card Sharps, Dream Books, and Bucket Shops: Gambling in Nineteenth-Century America*. Ithaca, NY: Cornell University Press, 1990.

Fenby, Jonathan. *Generalissimo: Chiang Kai-shek and the China He Lost*. London: Free Press, 2003.

Field, Bryan."Dark Discovery Beats Alsab by Length in Stake." *New York Times*, October 22, 1942.

———. "Dark Discovery Second, Level Best Holds On to Win Coaching Club Oaks by a Neck." *New York Times*, June 1, 1941.

———. "Favorite Beats Dark Discovery." *New York Times*, October 1, 1941.

"Find Mystery in $46,000 of 'Coup Plotter.'" *Chicago Tribune*, November 26, 1934.

Finney, Humphrey S. *Fair Exchange: Recollections of a Life with Horses*. London: J. A. Allen, 1974.

Francis, Dick. *A Jockey's Life: The Biography of Lester Piggott*. New York: Fawcett Crest, 1986.

Friedlander, Paul. *Rock and Roll: A Social History*. Boulder, CO: Westview Press, 1996.

Frischauer, Willi. *The Aga Khans*. London: Bodley Head, 1970.

Gammon, Clive. "Call It the Sport of Sheikhs." *Sports Illustrated*, December 1, 1986.

———. "Horses for His Kingdom." *Sports Illustrated*, November 13, 1978.

Glass, Margaret. *The Calumet Story*. Lexington, KY: Calumet Farm, 1979.

Gordon, David."The Winter's Night They Took Shergar." *Belfast Telegraph*, May 31, 2003.

Gould, Jonathan. *Can't Buy Me Love: The Beatles, Britain, and America*. New York: Harmony Books, 2007.

Gould, Lewis L. *Reform and Regulation: American Politics from Roosevelt to Wilson*. Prospect Heights, IL: Waveland Press, 1996.

Grant, Peter. "Rock the Casbah—Liverpool Venue Where the Beatles Played First." *Liverpool Echo*, July 6, 2010.

Bibliography

Greenwall, Harry J. *His Highness the Aga Khan: Imam of the Ismailis.* London: Cresset Press, 1952.

Haight, Walter. "Horses and People." *Washington Post,* June 4, 1954.

Hales, Linda. "Aga Khan, Jet-Setting on a Higher Plane."*Washington Post,* January 26, 2005.

Hampson, Sarah. "Just One More Sip of Beatles Juice." *Globe and Mail* (Canada), November 5, 2005.

Harris, Bill. "Rock the Casbah: Birth of the Beatles Surfaces from Mrs. Best's Basement." *Toronto Sun,* August 17, 2003.

Hertsgaard, Mark. *A Day in the Life: The Music and Artistry of the Beatles.* New York: Macmillan, 1995.

Hollingsworth, Kent. *The Kentucky Thoroughbred.* Lexington: University Press of Kentucky, 1976.

———. *The Wizard of the Turf: John E. Madden of Hamburg Place.* Lexington, KY: Blood-Horse, 1965.

"Horse's Owners Reject Talks with Abductors." *New York Times,* February 11, 1983.

Hughes, Albion. "Once More—It's a Son of Nasrullah." *Sports Illustrated,* October 18, 1954.

———. "Two for Clark: A Little-Known American Has Now Won Both the Derby and the St. Leger." *Sports Illustrated,* September 20, 1954.

Hughes, Mark. "Shergar and a Twenty-five Year Mystery." *Independent* (London), February 5, 2008.

Hughes, Robert. "The Nation's Grand New Showcase." *Time,* May 8, 1978.

"International Laurels." *Time,* October 27, 1952.

"Isaac M. Singer's Will: Decision of the Surrogate—Mrs. Foster Not the Widow of the Millionaire." *Chicago Tribune,* January 13, 1876.

"J. E. Madden Dies by Shot in Kentucky: County Patrol Chief Says Son of Horseman Was a Suicide." *New York Times,* February 27, 1943.

James, Jeremy. *The Byerly Turk: The Incredible Story of the World's First Thoroughbred.* Mechanicsburg, PA: Stackpole Books, 2005.

Jennings, Frank. "You, Too, May Win an Epsom Derby." *Thoroughbred Record,* June 12, 1954.

"John A. Bell Dead." *New York Times,* February 27, 1933.

"John A. Bell Gets Appeal." *New York Times,* May 25, 1926.

"John A. Bell Paroled." *New York Times*, July 26, 1929.

"John Bell Is Held as Bank Embezzler: Pennsylvania Authorities on 14 Counts Charge Misappropriation of $800,643." *New York Times*, August 5, 1925.

Johnson, William. "Doctor Beauty Buys a Beast." *Sports Illustrated*, February 19, 1968.

Kieran, John. "On the Epsom Downs." *New York Times*, June 1, 1932.

"Larkspur Posts Dramatic Triumph at Epsom Derby." *Schenectady (NY) Gazette*, June 7, 1962.

Leggett, William. "O.K., Bring On the Boys." *Sports Illustrated*, November 17, 1975.

Leigh, Spencer. *The Beatles in Hamburg: The Stories, the Scene and How It All Began.* Chicago: Chicago Review Press, 2011.

Lennox, Muriel. *Dark Horse: Unraveling the Mystery of Nearctic.* Toronto: Beach House Books, 2001.

———. *The Horse and the Tiger.* Toronto: Beach House Books, 2010.

Levin, Jason. *From the Desert to the Derby: The Ruling Family of Dubai's Billion-Dollar Quest to Win America's Greatest Horse Race.* New York: Daily Racing Form Press, 2001.

Long, Tania. "Richards' Mount, 5–1, Beats Queen's Aureole in Classic." *New York Times*, June 7, 1953.

Lyle, R. C. *The Aga Khan's Horses.* London: Putnam-London, 1938.

Magnum, William Preston, II. *A Kingdom for the Horse: A Classic Epic of the Brightest Star in American Race Horse Breeding History.* Louisville, KY: Harmony House Publishing, 1999.

Martin, George. *All You Need Is Ears.* New York: St. Martin's Press, 1979.

Mathiu, Paul. *The Masters of Manton: From Alec Taylor to George Todd.* London: Write First Time, 2010.

"Max Hirsch, 88, Who Trained Three Kentucky Derby Winners, Dies." *New York Times*, April 3, 1969.

McCreary, James Bennett. "Memoires." Unpublished manuscript in the author's possession.

Mearns, Dan. *Seattle Slew.* Lexington, KY: Eclipse Press, 2000.

Mellon, Paul. *Reflections in a Silver Spoon.* New York: William Morrow, 1992.

Middleton, Drew. "Never Say Die, 33–1, Defeats Arabian Night in Epsom Derby." *New York Times*, June 3, 1954.

Miles, Barry. *Paul McCartney: Many Years from Now*. London: Secker and Warburg, 1997.

"Mill Reef Wins Derby for Mellon." *Washington Post*, June 3, 1971.

"A Millionaire's Wives." *Chicago Tribune*, November 1, 1875.

Montgomery, Sue. "Sangster, Revolutionary International Breeder and Champion Owner, Dies at 67." *Independent* (London), April 9, 2004.

Moorhouse, Edward. *The History and Romance of the Derby*. London: Biographical Press, 1911.

Mortimer, Roger. *The History of the Derby Stakes*. London: Cassell, 1962.

Nack, William. *Secretariat: The Making of a Champion*. New York: Da Capo Press, 1975.

Nasaw, David. *Andrew Carnegie*. New York: Penguin Books, 2006.

Nelson, Michael. *Queen Victoria and the Discovery of the Riviera*. London: I. B. Tauris, 2001.

Nicholson, James C. *The Kentucky Derby: How the Run for the Roses Became America's Premier Sporting Event*. Lexington: University Press of Kentucky, 2012.

"Nijinsky Sweeps Irish Sweeps." *Ocala (FL) Star Banner*, June 28, 1970.

"Nijinsky Termed Wonder." *Calgary Herald*, October 1, 1970.

"Nijinsky Will Stand in Kentucky." *Spartanburg (SC) Herald-Journal*, August 16, 1970.

"Nijinsky Wins English Derby." *Washington Post*, June 4, 1970.

O'Connor, Harvey. *Mellon's Millions: The Biography of a Fortune: The Life and Times of Andrew W. Mellon*. New York: John Day, 1933.

Ours, Dorothy. *Man o' War: A Legend Like Lightning*. New York: St. Martin's Press, 2006.

Paphides, Pete. "Baby, You Can Drive My Van." *Times* (London), October 27, 2008.

"Pennsylvania Banks—6 Million Deposits—Close: Stagnation in the Coal Fields Blamed." *Chicago Tribune*, April 28, 1925.

Piggott, Lester. *Lester: The Autobiography of Lester Piggott*. London: Partridge Press, 1995.

Piggott, Lester, and Sean Magee. *Lester's Derbys*. London: Methuen, 2004.

"A Plot without Plotters." *Time*, December 3, 1934.

"Princeton Confers 624 Degrees Today." *New York Times*, June 17, 1941.

"Prison for Bank Wrecker." *New York Times*, May 19, 1927.

Pritchard, David, and Alan Lysaght. *The Beatles: An Oral History.* New York: Hyperion, 1998.

Richmond, Tom. "Memories of How the Late, Great Shergar Cruised to Victory with a Wonderful Record-Breaking Display in the 1981 Epsom Derby." *Yorkshire Post*, May 30, 2011.

Riess, Steven A. *The Sport of Kings and the Kings of Crime: Horse Racing, Politics, and Organized Crime in New York, 1865–1913.* Syracuse, NY: Syracuse University Press, 2011.

Riley, Tim. *Lennon: The Man, the Myth, the Music—The Definitive Life.* New York: Hyperion, 2011.

Roach, James. "Hopeful Goes to Battlefield as Saratoga's Meeting Ends." *New York Times*, August 27, 1950.

Robertson, William H. P. *The History of Thoroughbred Racing in America.* Englewood Cliffs, NJ: Prentice-Hall, 1964.

Robinson, Patrick, and Nick Robinson. *Horsetrader: Robert Sangster and the Rise and Fall of the Sport of Kings.* London: HarperCollins, 1994.

Ross, Nancy L. "Races Take the Guess out of Guest." *Washington Post*, November 12, 1968.

Roundtree, B. Seebohm, ed. *Betting and Gambling: A National Evil.* New York: Macmillan, 1905.

Ryan, Pat. "A Man of Arts and Letters." *Sports Illustrated*, March 16, 1970.

———. "The Walking Conglomerate." *Sports Illustrated*, April 28, 1969.

Scanlan, Lawrence. *The Horse God Built: The Untold Story of Secretariat, the World's Greatest Race Horse.* New York: St. Martin's Press, 2007.

"Scarlet Spots." *Time*, August 7, 1939.

Scatonit, Frank R., ed. *Finished Lines: A Collection of Memorable Writing in Thoroughbred Racing.* New York: DRF Press, 2002.

Schaffner, Nicholas S. *The Beatles Forever: How They Changed Our Culture.* New York: MJF Books, 1978.

Schmidt, Hans. *Maverick Marine: General Smedley D. Butler and the*

Contradictions of American Military History. Lexington: University Press of Kentucky, 1987.

Schmitz, David. "Fifty Years of Nasrullah." *Blood-Horse*, July 9, 2001.

———. "Man of Racing." *Blood-Horse*, February 10, 2007.

Seth-Smith, Michael, and Roger Mortimer. *Derby 200: The Official Story of the Blue Riband of the Turf.* Enfield, U.K.: Guinness Superlatives, 1979.

"Seven Horses Hit Dirt as Larkspur Wins Race." *Pittsburgh Post-Gazette*, June 7, 1962.

Shah, Sultan Muhammad, the Third Aga Khan. *The Memories of Aga Khan: World Enough and Time.* London: Cassell, 1954.

"The Show at Epsom Downs." *Time*, June 14, 1954.

Simpson, Janice C., J. D. Reed, and Jef McAllister. "Breeders, Place Your Bets." *Time*, August 23, 1982.

"The Singer Manufacturing Company: A Vast and Wonderful Organization." *New York Times*, January 1, 1886.

"Singer the Sewer." *Chicago Tribune*, May 9, 1875, 5.

"Sir Ivor Wins Race, $289,000 for Diplomat." *St. Petersburg (FL) Times*, May 30, 1968.

Slot, Owen. "I'll Never Forget That Night . . . the IRA Led Shergar into the Box without a Problem." *Telegraph* (London), June 2, 2001.

Smith, Marshall. "The People's Horse." *Life Magazine*, September 21, 1953.

Smith, Pohla. *Citation.* Lexington, KY: Eclipse Press, 2003.

"Son of J. E. Madden Ends Life in Store." *New York Times*, November 1, 1932.

Sounes, Howard. *Fab: An Intimate Life of Paul McCartney.* Cambridge, MA: Da Capo Press, 2010.

"Spectacular Bid Brings Record Syndication Figure." *Fredericksburg (VA) Free Lance-Star*, March 12, 1980.

Spitz, Bob. *The Beatles: The Biography.* New York: Little, Brown, 2005.

Standiford, Les. *Meet You in Hell: Andrew Carnegie, Henry Clay Frick, and the Bitter Partnership That Transformed America.* New York: Random House, 2005.

Stine, Gerald. "Roberto on Deck for 'Darby' Hit." *Washington Post*, June 5, 1972.

Stone, Richard. *Belmont Park: A Century of Champions.* Lexington, KY: Blood-Horse Publications, 2005.

Sue, Eugene. *The Godolphin Arabian*. Translated and adapted by Alex de Jonge. Lanham, MD: Derrydale Press, 2004.

"Syndicate Buys Nijinsky for Record $5.4 Million." *New York Times*, August 16, 1970.

Tesio, Federico. *Breeding the Racehorse*. London: J. A. Allen, 1968.

Thayer, Bert Clark. *Whirlaway: The Life and Times of a Great Racer*. New York: Abercrombie and Fitch, 1966.

Tower, Whitney. "Banana Nose Shows 'em How." *Sports Illustrated*, November 15, 1954.

———. "Cousin Leslie Goes to Market." *Sports Illustrated*, July 21, 1969.

———. "Even the Very Best Can Blunder." *Sports Illustrated*, October 26, 1970.

———. "The Man, the Horse, and the Deal That Made History." *Sports Illustrated*, June 1, 1959.

———. "Nashua's Sire and Mr. Fitz." *Sports Illustrated*, November 1, 1954.

———. "The Racing Doctor Made the Right Prognosis." *Sports Illustrated*, October 14, 1968.

———. "Saints and Sidewalks." *Sports Illustrated*, June 15, 1970.

———. "Showing Them a Thing or Two." *Sports Illustrated*, October 11, 1971.

Towers-Clark, Peter. "Mill Reef Flays the European Opposition." *Thoroughbred Record*, June 12, 1971.

———. "Roberto Extended the String." *Thoroughbred Record*, June 17, 1972.

Tracy, Len. "Yankee Victory." *Thoroughbred Record*, June 12, 1954.

Turner Publishing, ed. *Jockey's Guild—History of Race Riding*. New York: Turner Publishing, 1999.

"Two Banks Closed; Deposits $6,000,000." *New York Times*, April 28, 1925.

"Upperville's Never Say Die Wins Derby in England." *Washington Post*, June 3, 1954.

"U.S. Colt Takes St. Leger; Owner, 78, Weeps for Joy." *New York Times*, September 12, 1954.

"U.S.-Owned Horse Takes Epsom Derby." *Los Angeles Times*, June 7, 1962.

"U.S. Racer Is First in English Classic: R. S. Clark's Galatea II, 6–1

Shot, Triumphs with Ease in the 1,000 Guineas." *New York Times*, April 29, 1939.

Varola, Franco. *The Tesio Myth*. London: J. A. Allen, 1984.

"Virginian Gives $700,000 Horse to British Stud." *Washington Post*, May 26, 1956.

Walker, Alan Yuill. *Grey Magic: The Enigma of the Grey Thoroughbred*. Compton, U.K.: Highdown, 2005.

Wall, Maryjean. *How Kentucky Became Southern: A Tale of Outlaws, Gamblers, Horsethieves, and Breeders*. Lexington: University Press of Kentucky, 2010.

Walling, George Washington. *Recollections of a New York Chief of Police*. New York: Claxton Book Concern, 1887.

Wallis, Michael. *Oil Man: The Story of Frank Phillips and the Birth of Phillips Petroleum*. New York: Doubleday, 1988.

Weber, Nicholas Fox. *The Clarks of Cooperstown: Their Singer Sewing Machine Fortune, Their Great and Influential Art Collections, Their Forty-Year Feud*. New York: Alfred A. Knopf, 2007.

White, Dan. *Kentucky Bred: A Celebration of Thoroughbred Breeding*. Dallas: Taylor Publishing, 1986.

"The Wow Horse Races into History." *Time*, June 11, 1973.

Wright, Howard. *Bull: The Biography*. Halifax, U.K.: Timeform, 1995.

Wright, Jade. "Pete Best: I Feel I'm the Luckiest out of All the Beatles." *Liverpool Echo*, November 24, 2008.

Zachary, G. Pascal. "Do Business and Islam Mix? Ask Him." *New York Times*, July 8, 2007.

Index

Page numbers in *italics* refer to illustrations.

Index

Bernardini (horse), 173
Berry, Chuck, 7–9, 11
Best, Mona, xi, 7–8, 10–11, 131, 136, 162, 180n14
Best, Pete, 7–11, 105, 136–37, 162, 177
Black Selima (horse), 188n11
Blenheim (horse), 64–67, 73–74, 78, 121, 134–35, 155
Blue Sail (horse), 130
Blushing Groom (horse), 158, 160, 196n17, 197n25
Bold Ruler (horse), 84
Bold Venture (horse), 99
Boreale (horse), 46
Boyer, Isabella, 27
Breasley, Scobie, 121, 192n4
Breeders' Cup, 133, 167, 175, 197n27
Bridget (horse), 2
British Broadcasting Company (BBC), 3, 7, 162
Brown, Ken, 8, 180n14
Brownstown Stud, 81
Bull, Phil, 81, 121–22
Bunbury, Charles, 2, 68, 176
Burgoyne, John, 2
Business Plot, 42–43
Butler, Smedley D., 42
Butters, Frank, 80

Calumet Farm, 66–67, 73
Camelot (horse), 174–75
Candy Stripes (horse), 197n17
Carlburg Stables, 111, 118
Carmarthen (horse), 140
Carnegie Coal Company, 91
Carnegie Trust Company, 93–94
Casbah Coffee Club, xi, 8, 10
Catnip (horse), 75
Chalk Stream (horse), 153
Challacombe (horse), 115
Champagne Stakes, 99
Champion Stakes, 80, 143
Charles II (king), 2, 126
Chase, The (horse), 124–25
Chateaugay (horse), 151
Chatteris Stakes, 80

Cherokee Run (horse), 145
Chinn, Phil T., 99
Churchill, Winston, 1
Citation (horse), 83–84
Claiborne Farm, 66, 67, 72, 79, 82–83, 179n5, 188n11
Clark, Alfred Corning, 31, 33
Clark, Edward, 13, 20–21, 28, 30–31, 162
Clark, Francine Clary, 37–39, 41
Clark, Robert Sterling: and art collecting, 31, 33, 36–39, 149; birth and childhood, 33; and the Boxer Rebellion, 5, 34, 35; and "Business Plot," 42–43; China expedition, 36; and horse racing, 40–41, 43, 45–46, 81, 87, 108, 111, 117, 126, 129–34, 138; in Paris, 36–38; and sibling rivalry, 36–37, 39; and the Spanish-American War, 5, 13; in the U.S. Department of War, 35; in World War I, 37
Clark, Stephen C., 36–37, 39
Clemente, Roberto, 150–51, 195n26
Coaching Club American Oaks, 100
Cochran, Eddie, 7, 180n11
Comstock Lode, 99
Connaught (horse), 138
Consolidated Edison, 70
Coolmore Stud, 154, 161, 163–64, 167–68, 172–75
Cooperstown, NY, 30, 33–34, 39, 150
Cope, Alfred, 130–31
Coronation Stakes, 64
Count Fleet (horse), 67
Coventry Stakes, 80
Croker, Richard "Boss," 179n5
Cromwell, Tomas B., 97
Crow, William E., 92–93
Curd, Andy, 88
Current (horse), 40, 184n8

Dakota (building), 30, 162
Daley, Marcus, 104
Dalham Hall Stud, 164
Danehill (horse), 172
Danzig (horse), 173

212

Index

Index

Index

Lukas, D. Wayne, 168
Lyphard (horse), 197n25

MacDonald, Ramsay, 73
Madden, J. Edward, 107
Madden, John E., 99, 104, 105–7, *106*
Madden, Joseph, 107
Magliano, Theresa "Ginetta," 56–57, 64
Magnier, John, 153–55
Mahmoud (horse), 65, 77–79, *78*, 118, 121, 130, 135
Maktoum, Mohammed bin Rashid Al, 145, 147, 164–66, 168, 170–71, 173, 176, 195n24, 198n31, 198n32
Man o' War (horse), 46, 119, 121
Manton training yard, 111–18, 153
Marr, Marnie, 101
Martin, George, 10
Matthias, John, 162
McCartney, Paul, 8–11, 136, 180n11
McCreary, James Bennett, 101, 190n17
McElligott, Gerald, 46, 127, 188n22
McGonigal, Mary, 25
McGrath, Joseph, 81, 188n22
Medaglia d'Oro (horse), 173
Meddler (horse), 69–70, 188n11
Mellon, Andrew W., 41–42, 90, 93, *95*
Mellon, Paul, 140, 143–45, 148, *149*
Mercer, Manny, 121, 127, 192n3
Merritt Players, 18
Meydan racecourse, 170
Miesque (horse), 175
Mill Reef (horse), 144–45, 150
Mill Ridge Farm, 139, 194n10
Minstrel, The (horse), 156–57, 160–61
Mr. Prospector (horse), 175
Mumtaz Begum (horse), 74, 77, 79
Mumtaz Mahal (horse), 63–64, 74, 78–79, 121, 150, 155
Mussolini, Benito, 76

Nad al Sheba racecourse, 170
Nashua (horse), 83, *84*, 85
Nashwan (horse), 196n17
Nasrullah (horse), 6, 46–47, 79–81, 83–87, 111, 119, 125, 134, 139,
144, 150, 154, 174, 188n22, 196n17
Nassau Stakes, 114
National Society for the Prevention of Cruelty to Children, 112
National Stud (English), 133, 145, 193n22
Nazi Party, 77
Nearco, 74–77, 79, 81, 119, 121, 150, 152, 155
Never Say Die (horse): arrival in England, 111; birth, 88–89; breaking, 110; Phil Bull's commentary on, 121–22; conformation, 119–20; in Derby, 129–31; Derby preparation, 127–29; early life, 107–9; first race, 120; first stakes start, 121; first start as a three-year-old, 126; in King Edward VII Stakes, 131; retirement, 132–34; in Richmond Stakes, 121; as a stallion, 135; in St. Leger Stakes, 132
Never Too Late (horse), 193n1
Newmarket, 61, 63, 70, 76, 80, 111, 118–21, 123, 126–27, 129, 132–33, 143, 156, 164, 192n6
New Stakes, 120
Niarchos, Stavros, 175
Nijinsky (horse), 140–44, 150, 152, 154–56, 168, *169*, 174, 194n23, 195n25
Nijinsky, Romola, 141
Nizam Gold Cup, 52
Nizari Islam. *See* Ismaili Muslims
Nobiliary (horse), 157, 196n11
Nogara (horse), 75
Noor (horse), 83–84
Northern Dancer (horse), 78, 155–56, 161, 163–65, 197n23

Oaks Stakes. *See* English Oaks
O'Brien, Aiden, 174, 198n33
O'Brien, Joseph, 174, 198n33
O'Brien, Vincent, 135, 138, 140, 142, 150, 152–56, 158, 160, 163, 168
Oldway Mansion, 28, *28–29*, 115, 182n27

Index

Index

Index